AWAKENING HEART

ALSO BY ANDREW MARSHALL

The Great Little Book of Happiness

AWAKENING HEART

THE BLISSFUL PATH TO SELF-REALISATION

Andrew Marshall

RADIANT SUN BOOKS

First published in 2011 by Radiant Sun Books

30 Haywood Grange
Little Haywood
Stafford
ST18 0UB

www.radiantsunbooks.com

ISBN: 978-0-955-93641-8

A CIP catalogue record for this book is available from the British Library.

Cover design by Dan Prescott

Typography and typesetting by Couper Street Type Co.
www.couperstreet.com

Prepared and printed by:
York Publishing Services Ltd
64 Hallfield Road
Layerthorpe
York YO31 7ZQ

ACKNOWLEDGEMENTS

Thank you . . .

This book didn't just happen but came together over a period of time. Heartfelt thanks go to my wife, Gloria, for always being there and supporting me throughout, and to all those friends who have participated in and encouraged the work that we both do.

I am deeply indebted to Claire Wingfield, who has demonstrated great perspicacity in polishing my very rough manuscript with her vast editorial knowledge and skill; and, although it is said you cannot tell a book by its cover, appearance is important, and it has been a delight to have had Dan Prescott creating the cover and page designs.

Finally, and most importantly, none of this work could have been written without the long line of teachers in many traditions who, for thousands of years, have inspired humanity to follow the heart. I have tried to be true to that teaching but, I hope it goes without saying, any faults in the following pages are entirely mine.

{ CONTENTS

INTRODUCTION

Today, perhaps more than at any other time, there is a great search going on. We appear irrevocably immersed in consumerism, thirsty for ever-more sophisticated technology to satisfy our demands for easy living or amusement. Yet we all know, deep down, that these desires can never be permanently fulfilled – just put on hold for a while, merely to resurface in another form.

In order to be truly fulfilled, we need to express ourselves utterly and completely. This means uncovering our true essence and allowing it to blossom. Until, in effect, we *become* that essence – the most natural expression of which is *love*.

There is an enormous need for love, both in our individual lives and in the world as a whole, and love can only flourish in humanity if it blossoms in the heart of each of us. *Awakening Heart* is about following the most natural path to our true nature or essence. By learning to love fully and completely, and by living with full awareness in the present moment, we can become totally fulfilled, and truly happy, human beings.

The blissful path of the heart begins with *unlearning* many of the beliefs that society has built around love – beliefs that condition most of the human population. To do this, we need to be able to distinguish between true love and the emotions that are often identified as love, but which eventually only cause pain. More importantly, we need to transform the way we think: so that we can overcome the barriers that prevent us from feeling love fully – the internal barriers of indifference and negativity. By cultivating the qualities of the heart, the elixir of life is able to course through our whole being, leading to the bliss that comes with self-realisation.

Awakening Heart is about the very unscientific elements of fire, water, air and earth, which are not elements at all as a chemist understands them, but principles. An engineer can craft the most marvellous sports coupé, speedboat or space rocket; or an instrument maker can create a wonderful violin, trumpet or guitar, but all such things are dead objects unless some life is breathed into them. We are the same. *Awakening Heart* is about the love, warmth and feeling that give brightness to life and the understanding that where there is brightness there are also shadows. This is a book about life with passion and yet life which has extraordinary stillness and clarity. It is about how to become a warrior; a warrior who would not harm even the smallest insect but who lives a life of inner strength and peacefulness.

Here is an invitation to take part in an adventure. A journey that is perhaps the most important any of us can ever make; a voyage of self-discovery that leads to the very core of our being.

1

THE MAGICAL RADIANCE OF THE HEART

THE HEART-SUN

Deep within every human being, is a magical source of warmth sometimes known as the *heart-sun*. Its location in the body is within the centre of the chest, a little to the right of the heart. But that is only its physical location. If a corpse were dissected, no-one would be able to find the heart-sun because the corpse is only tissue, fluid and bones. The heart-sun isn't composed of tissue or any other physical aspect of the human being.

We might say that when we feel love for someone the heart-sun is shining, but that is only part of the picture. There is much more to it than that. Like the sun in the sky, the heart-sun can become obscured, and in some of us the clouds of the mind and emotions are very strong and far-reaching. Just as if hidden by an overcast sky, the heart-sun may seem to be absent and we may think it buried forever or question its very existence. Yet even when seemingly covered, the heart-sun provides nourishment, so that in each of us there is heat and light. But how much stronger and more enriching that warmth and brightness can be when we begin to clear the haze. All we have to do is provide the right conditions for these wonderful qualities to flourish, awakening the heart-sun so that life is filled with richness, with warmth, with colour and with light. There is no need to go anywhere to do this – the heart-sun is right here, right now and just needs uncovering, or maybe it is fairly bright already but there is still a lot of haze. Either way, all of us can enrich this beautiful world of ours and radiate warmth and richness to everyone around us. The secret to this is the essence of the heart centre, the magic of the heart-sun. Your natural state, your true nature, is truly magnificent. Radiance is natural and should be a normal part of life. The only thing preventing its expression is our emotional and mental make-up, which is like a veneer superimposed on top.

Awakening the heart to a life of vitality is to be prepared to breathe some fresh air into the dusty old books; to bring some fire, passion and warmth into life; and to have the stillness and confidence that comes with truly knowing yourself. That is what the awakened heart-sun – the source of life at the core of our being – will do for all of us, if only we let it. Then it will become the Fiery Heart.

THE ELIXIR OF LIFE

There have always been tales and legends of an elixir that brings everlasting youthfulness and many people have spent precious years trying to find it. Even today, vast sums are spent by consumers on this product or that in the rather vain hope that they will become as fresh and young as a new daisy in the morning dew. Perhaps they do receive a temporary lift of some sort or the other but daisies, you may have noticed, don't stay fresh and young for very long either.

Rather than searching out exotic substances and compounds to ingest or apply to the body, which handsomely line the pockets of those who market them, we might turn our attention to how the mind affects the body and our sense of well-being. A mind that is aggressive, for example, wears the body out more quickly than one that is calm. If we are in a negative state, worrying or fearful perhaps, notice how our sense of well-being takes a nosedive. Our thoughts have a very definite affect on the body's responses. What good is some magic herb, potion or serum then? When the mind and its reactions are the cause of most of our troubles, anything we ingest or apply to the body in the hope of it looking younger can only have a superficial effect.

But what can we make of tales of an elixir? Might it be that if the mind is the cause of producing many of the body's aging compounds, the mind may also be capable of maintaining, or at least prolonging, a more youthful state?

The Chinese regard chi, the vital energy of the body, as an elixir. They talk of the "lower dan tian", a centre in the abdomen just below the navel, as being the ocean of elixir because chi can build up very strongly there. There are hundreds if not thousands of specific exercises that can help to increase chi and, apart from the physical movements, the mind is also very important in this process. An exercise carried out with full awareness may encourage the build-up of chi but the same exercise done inattentively or carelessly will have little effect. People in whom the chi is strong and well-balanced tend to maintain strength, vitality and mobility for much longer than those whose chi is poorly developed or out of balance.

The Chinese also refer to "jing"[1], which is closely related to chi and regarded as the body's essence. Volumes have been written about these concepts, but for us, for the moment, it is sufficient to appreciate that there is a long-held understanding that the co-operation of mind, body and breath can build up our energy and improve the quality of life. That increase of energy and quality of life is sometimes attributed to an elixir that is produced within the body. At a physical or clinical level, this "elixir" may be attributed to enzymes, hormones or biochemicals secreted by various glands. It remains crucial that awareness or consciousness plays a role in contributing to this process.

Ayurveda, the ancient Indian system of health which is also rooted in consciousness, also seems to refer to an elixir in the production of "ojas"[2]. Ojas is said to be a very fine substance or secretion that arises through a combination of wholesome diet, wholesome activity and, most importantly, a wholesome state of consciousness. Certain factors can

---

1 For a full explanation of jing and the significance of awareness in the cultivation of chi, see *Qigong Meditation – Embryonic Breathing* Dr Yang, Jwing-Ming, YMAA Publication Center.

2 There is an enormous amount of material available on Ayurveda. See, for example, *Textbook of Ayurveda – Fundamental Principles* Dr Vasant Lad, The Ayurvedic Press.

reduce this – tiredness, coarse speech, coarse thinking, excesses of any kind and anything that is unwholesome, for example. When ojas is present, it is said to give radiance to the complexion, a feeling of ease and sometimes the experience of bliss in the body. There is also reference within this tradition to a substance called "soma". A literal interpretation of the Rig Veda would give the understanding that soma is a herb, or a substance extracted from a herb, that is the "drink of the gods". A more intuitive interpretation is that soma is something produced within the body which arises as a result of a state of consciousness – an internal elixir.

HEART ESSENCE – THE SUPER ELIXIR

Cultivation of the qualities of the heart produces dramatic changes in life. Life simply becomes better when we love. It's a message which has become distorted over time into all sorts of half truths and often into complete aberrations. How to develop those heart qualities will be the subject of closer inspection later in this book, but for now let's think of one of the remarkable by-products of love. The body's chemistry changes as our moods change and the most beneficial effects arise when the mind is at its most positive. Just look at the radiance in the face of someone who loves and you will see that something in the heart is making the countenance glow. Look at the eyes and see the sparkle. These are real bodily effects. Love makes us younger; there's no doubt about it. Love produces an elixir. Love increases the flow of chi in the body; it lowers blood pressure and increases our sense of well-being. The immune system becomes stronger because we are happier and so sickness results less often. Everything about the body works better when a person expresses love in its true sense.[3]

The natural radiance of a person who truly and deeply loves is very similar to that arising from ojas or from chi, almost as though the heart centre exudes some special secretion which causes the body to function at its optimum. Gradually, we can develop the skill to produce this wonderful substance which arises not from any physical effort but from a very natural, if perhaps rather special, attitude to life. Whatever the biochemical constituents are is not important, nor does it matter for us whether there is one super-substance that is the heart elixir or the play of a combination of factors. The driver of a motor car doesn't need to know the constituents of fuel but does need to know how to put the right quality of fuel into the car.

RADIANCE AND THE ENERGY EFFECT

Love has a direct bearing on radiance. For most of us, love is something that we feel towards a member of our family or towards a close friend. To think in terms of selfless love

---

3 There has been much research on the physiological effects of love and will undoubtedly be much more. For an overview of some of this research, see *The Health Benefits of Love,* M. Langton November 2007.

towards people we don't know very well may seem unnecessary. But the effects on our own life of doing precisely that are extraordinary.

Each one of us has a certain amount of protective space which we have built around us, called a "comfort zone". Provided nothing threatens that comfort zone, we are fine. We have many comfort zones, some of which relate to how we act in certain circumstances and some simply to how we maintain distance from other people. A comfort zone provides a limit on how far we are prepared to extend our energy – and to a certain extent, too, how far we are prepared to receive energy from others.

When a comfort zone is threatened, the radiance from our own energy starts to withdraw. There is a "turning in" while we subconsciously draw the energy back towards us. As that happens, the amount of available energy for us to act is lowered. Extraordinary though it is, our habitual tendency to defend ourselves through our mental and emotional responses frequently works against us rather than for us. Sometimes, of course, some level of protection or some defence mechanism is desirable or even necessary. If we have injured ourselves, for example, we naturally guard against the injury being touched or knocked. At a more subtle level, an emotional trauma will usually result in some guardedness against anything that may carry the risk of further emotional pain. Either way, the result is that our energy is not fully available – for ourselves or for others – and so to live life fully it is important that we restore our energy as soon as we can.

Few people truly realise the extraordinary potential of their energy. Some of us realise much of it much of the time but rather like the mesembryanthemum flower that closes up when the sun goes in, we are a little picky. Under certain circumstances we shine but when the conditions change, we close up – sometimes partially and at other times completely – and we lose out. Our energy level drops and the "feel-good factor" disappears. Of course, this isn't really how we want to be. We need to learn how to reverse the tendency towards unnecessary self-protection so that gradually we have more and more energy, more and more of the feel-good factor and more and more joy in our lives.

THE AWFUL TRUTH ABOUT A LIFE WITHOUT RADIANCE

Life without radiance is full of fog. It is dull and unproductive. The only good point about it is that once we realise that we are immersed in dullness, there is just one way to go and that is into increasing brightness. But it is a mistake to think that a dull life in this sense means one that is necessarily inactive or boring.

A person may be very active socially, going to all manner of gatherings and have a keen interest in the latest gossip about everyone on the social scene. Some would say that is far from dull but unless other qualities are present, in terms of radiance that person may be very dull indeed. Instead of giving out warmth and kindness, they are actually sucking in and feeding off others. To feed off gossip is a very negative mental state because inevitably it is judgemental and divisive.

It also fritters away energy. A gossip is like a pot full of holes; it contains little, and what it does hold leaks out and makes a mess.

Someone may run a successful business, working all hours and making a fine profit. That is hardly dull in the conventional sense and there are many radiant souls running successful businesses. But if the aim of the business is solely to provide profit or meet selfish ends, no matter how active or highly motivated the person is, there is almost certainly a lack of radiance. Is the business carried out happily and benefiting the community in some way? Are the staff well-paid and looked after, the customers treated with kindness and respect? Is the business run with kindness as well as with acumen? Or does the business prosper and benefit from the misfortune of others or by making life difficult for rivals or suppliers?

Perhaps we are very busy looking after someone less fortunate than us. Caring for another is a marvellous opportunity for increasing the radiance of the heart-sun because although the work may be hard and unrewarding financially, the correct mental attitude can produce huge rewards for us *inside*. But if we give that care simply because we have to, out of a sense of duty and maybe at times with a little resentment or while feeling sorry for ourselves, our sun is hidden by dark clouds. If we are a paid carer and do it just because it is a job, we are dull. In fact, whatever our role in life, if we do it simply because we have to and trudge along from one day to the next, perhaps looking forward to the next day off, our light is hidden.

A life without radiance has little love in it and very little expression of gratitude, appreciation or joy. Whether a person spends his or her waking time earning money, being idle or looking after other people, if any of these activities is pursued with little joy, that precious time is wasted. If we provide our services free of charge but dislike what we are doing, resent it or do it solely for recognition, we are a sunless person. Or perhaps we live solely for the purpose of self-satisfaction, merely for pleasure or self-indulgence, for acquiring things, money or power. There's some dynamism here, at least, but the energy flows in the wrong direction. If we are like that, we are like a black hole in space, sucking everything in.

To be a sunless person doesn't depend on activity so much because a radiant person may have the most mundane of lifestyles and responsibilities; what the radiant person has that their sunless friend lacks is the attitude and mental energy that makes their whole being radiate.

Sadly, today our society is full of sunless people.[4] Instead of allowing their inner radiance to shine, many people take solace from what they can take for themselves. Overconsumption is an acute symptom of this and is a serious problem manifesting in all sorts of ways, not just in obesity, alcoholism and other addictions. Instead of a 'take, take' society, we need one where generosity and

4 You may say, quite rightly, that few people can be totally sunless and totally without warmth because everyone has something in life that triggers a radiant response. But if one per cent of a person's waking hours are joyful and outgoing, it means that for 99% of the time, their energy is not radiating, that they are not enjoying life and not creating joy around them.

kindness rule the day. Waiting for others to change isn't the answer. Radiance results from selflessness, from providing support for others without seeking reward or recognition.

FULL BRILLIANCE COMES FROM ENLIGHTENMENT

Ideally we would radiate warmth and kindness constantly and at full beam, but the truth of the matter is that none of us can exhibit these qualities all the time. None of us is perfect; we all have mental and emotional flaws. Mental currents – our habitual thinking patterns and beliefs – cloud our perception and either stir up emotions or stultify them. In other words we are not superhuman, so the production of the wonderful elixir of the heart is necessarily limited. But need that be the case? Is it possible to become lighter and brighter, warmer and happier to such an extent that the mind and emotions become clear?

Clarity is an extraordinary quality. When something possesses clarity, light can shine through it. That might be in the physical sense, like light being able to shine through a clear window or lens, but it can also refer to something becoming known to us because the mind is clear enough to let that meaning come through. When something is unclear, it may be that the mind cannot grasp it as certain pathways in the mind are not open. Those pathways might require some new knowledge, aptitude, understanding or experience in order to be accessed.[5]

Sometimes we need to be shown how to open those pathways, which is the role of a teacher. In one sense, nobody truly teaches; a teacher merely facilitates the learner in opening up or developing his or her own faculties. The real importance of education is in opening up the pathways in human minds and altering perception and understanding; its imperfection is that it mainly relies on the transmission of facts or the acquisition of skills.[6]

There is a further way of looking at mental and emotional clarity. If the mind and emotions are absolutely clear (which also, incidentally, means they must be still), what do they allow to come through them? We can sometimes experience a moment when the mind has stopped wandering – no thoughts, no daydreams, no stirring of emotions; being wide awake like that in the present moment, what remains is *pure awareness*. Becoming more acquainted with pure awareness, and eventually establishing it as a normal part of life, is often called the process of enlightenment. Interestingly, the French word for enlightenment is *éclaircissement* – making clear. This process of clarifying the mind and emotions results in the possibility of a purer type of knowledge being

---

5 Such pathways can also sometimes become physically obstructed – simple tiredness can obstruct the operation of the mind, for example, as can alcohol and other substances that affect the brain and nervous system.

6 Education can allow chinks of light in but there can never be a state of *total* clarity arising from it. Always there will be something else to learn because nobody can know absolutely every fact or be skilful at everything that can be done. This is why, as the education of the individual grows, there tends to be an increase in specialisation.

able to enter the mind. *Purer* because it is untrammelled by the thinking mind with its morass of beliefs, prejudices, conceptions and thinking patterns. This knowledge is sometimes said to bring greater light into the mind, hence the word *enlightenment*.

So what has this to do with warmth and the production of heart elixir? In order for the mind to experience clarity, there has to be a certain amount of refinement of the nervous system. Even if the surface of water is still, if the water itself is polluted by mud, clarity is impossible; in a similar way, so it is with the nervous system. There also has to be refinement of the mind so that, for a time at least, it is free of the concepts that normally affect its perception. One of the things that we begin to understand when we make a little progress along the path to clarity is that our perception of others, of our environment and of ourselves is dependent upon our ever-fluctuating state of mind. With a little further progress, it may start to dawn upon us that we have a very deep-seated belief that everything is separate from us and that gives rise to all our mental and emotional discomfort, no matter how mild or strong. As we look deeper into our own nature, that sense of separateness begins very slowly to dissolve and in its place a sense of warmth and connectedness with everything around us gradually emerges. The greater the warmth that comes into life and the less separate we feel from everything and everyone, the more the heart-sun opens and so the elixir of the heart can be produced.

With greater clarity of mind and the development of warmth into what eventually becomes all-encompassing loving kindness and compassion, a different quality of energy is experienced in both body and mind. In the body there will normally be a feeling of great well-being and the senses will support a greater or heightened level of awareness. At times this may be experienced as a sensation of bliss. The mind will be very stable and open. Pure awareness is natural and uncontrived. Some make the mistake of thinking that a clear mind means one that remains unmoving, with the consequence that they try to fabricate a false state of stillness which is constrained rather than open.[7] The truly clear mind is light as well as stable and has full awareness. With such a mind, the heart centre has enormous capacity. We will be exploring the potential this has both for us as individuals and for our society later in the book. At this point it is good to reflect that although enlightenment may seem a long process, any steps we make along the path unfold the natural goodness that lies within each of us. To do that, no matter how little, is very significant.

THE LOST MESSAGE OF RELIGION

Does religion have a function in this process of enlightenment? Many today would say not because they have found religion lacking in some way and yet they feel an inner draw to their spiritual nature, even though they may not describe it as such. Others will tell you that enlightenment is just a

---

7 A simple but effective meditation for calming the mind is set out in the Appendix.

new-age term for what religion is about, that all you need to do is follow the edicts of your chosen religion, have unshakeable faith and you will be saved from all your failings. There are others who say that they find deep and real comfort from their faith which they pursue in a quiet and often very private way.

Religion has its purpose. It can provide a structure with clearly defined ethics and there are cultures which are clearly structured around religion. That, we could say, is the outer aspect. There is also an inner aspect which requires faith or belief and it is this that is often objected to in this age where inner values are often greatly lacking. But religions do not begin with a structure of social rules nor do they start out with a demand to believe in scriptures or anything contained in them. In fact, religions do not start out with any structures or demands at all.

What is so often lacking in religion is a third aspect and that we could call the *innermost* aspect. Although those with extreme views assert that religion is created by God, a Supreme Being or the Divine for man to follow, all the tenets of any religion have actually been written down by human beings. Before any religion begins, there is someone who has discovered truth within himself or herself and, having made that discovery, shows others how to make that discovery for themselves. In other words, an enlightened individual teaches others the path to enlightenment according to the needs of those whom he or she teaches. What is right for one person is not necessarily right for another because everyone has different levels of understanding. Nevertheless, as time goes on, the guidance of that original teacher is passed on and written down by others whose level of understanding will not be as clear as the original teacher and so misunderstandings and misinterpretations arise. For one person it may be right to focus on behaving ethically, for another it may be more appropriate to develop intellectual understanding and for a third it may be that love and compassion is the best way to develop. There is no one path that is right for all. Those who follow their religion quietly and with much reflection find that, as their understanding and intuition develop, a literal interpretation of scriptures is not usually correct and a deeper meaning lies within.

It is the essence of the original teaching that often becomes lost, so that instead of helping individuals to overcome all prejudices and faults, religion has the opposite effect and entrenches them more deeply. One only has to listen to the fundamentalists of any faith and realise that their beliefs have made them more discriminating rather than less. This is not the fault of the religion; it is the failing of human minds.

If we look back at the essence of any religion, we will find that love is strongly present and it is the development of love, the natural quality of the heart, that evolves into compassion and enables the magical radiance of the heart to expand. Like the light and warmth from the sun, love does not discriminate between one class of person and another. Equally, discrimination and class have no part in the original essence of religion. There are no chosen ones; there are simply billions of people in this world with varying degrees of suffering and ignorance. By delving within and opening the heart, ignorance is gradually dispelled and so is suffering.

Whether we formally follow a religion or not is not

important. What matters is whether we can make the world a kinder, better, place simply by how we are and how we live. This requires a gradual overcoming of prejudice and a broadening of our mental horizons. It requires light in the mind and fire in the heart and what follows in this book is intended as an aid in achieving just that.

2

FAKE STUFF { THE TRUTH ABOUT 'I LOVE YOU'

WHAT LOVE CAN BE

Writing about love is in a way a most difficult thing to do because there are so many misunderstandings surrounding love and, inevitably, whatever one writes bears the possibility of being misinterpreted. Love is often associated with romance, with family relationships, with affairs, broken hearts – many scenarios which can form the setting for much emotional pain. But the painful experiences which every human being goes through at one time or another are not simply the result of love. As we shall look at shortly, it is human nature to have preconceptions and expectations about the behaviour of others and of our own needs; when these are not met or come crashing down, we can encounter a personal crisis which is inevitably painful. This is not the pain of love, though it is often confused for it.

The quality of love that this book explores and invites the reader to cultivate is one which rises, or indeed soars, above human foibles. Its quality or nature is so high, in fact, that it achieves many things that can rightfully be described as miraculous. Love is an extraordinary energy that is present throughout the universe. With it comes the extraordinary capacity to heal at every level because it unites and makes things whole. Love is limited only by our consciousness, narrowed as that is by our beliefs, fears, prejudices and emotional pain; fortunately, even those are healed or resolved as we allow ourselves to open to this wonderful and mysterious force.

WHAT LOVE IS

What love is, it is impossible to know fully or, indeed, to define, because love isn't solely the prerogative of humans and their field of experience. If it were, it might be easy, or relatively so, to define it. Love is universal and occurs in different ways according to the different conditions that exist. The love of a matriarchal elephant for the rest of the herd, protecting and nurturing, is likely to be very different in expression and experience from that of many human beings, for example. But nurturing and protecting are two aspects of love that we can understand and relate to.

We may occasionally come across the adage "God is love". Although children, not to mention many adults, might use the word "God" to refer to some almighty being that is separate from the rest of us, if we understand "God" to mean the totality of everything in, throughout and beyond the universe, both manifest and transcendent, love may then be understood as something more than an individual expression. It becomes an expression or an aspect of totality and so becomes cosmic or even super-cosmic in proportion. Love becomes limitless and expressible at every level and, rather beautifully, must be intrinsic in absolutely everything.

If we can understand love as some extraordinary, amazing energy or force that permeates the whole universe and beyond, that holds together, brings together, heals, forms and builds, then inevitably we must begin to understand that it is far more than sentiment or emotion. Love as we may experience it as human beings is only the most dilute expression of this cosmic energy. But, although love is inexhaustibly bigger than we are, it is possible to develop our capacity to express it, in the same way that any human ability or capacity can be developed.

The cosmic proportion of love is less easy to comprehend or imagine because it is totally beyond our experience and knowledge. However, we might be able to grasp the fact that, if love is everywhere throughout the cosmos, it cannot apply to some things and not others. "Universal" means what it says. We will look at this more deeply later in the book. For now, we need to bring ourselves firmly back to earth and to do so it will be useful for us to look at some of the emotions that are often mistaken for love. Because we mistake them for love, we often cause ourselves pain and there are few people, if any, on the planet who have not experienced them. These emotions look like love and feel like love but are fake, just like fool's gold.

HOW TO RECOGNISE WHEN WE ARE FAKING IT

There is nothing wrong with iron pyrites. If you remember chemistry lessons from your schooldays, you may recall that iron pyrites has a gold appearance, is shiny and quite pleasing to the eye. So realistic can its appearance be that it often fooled gold prospectors of old into believing they had found the real thing. Probably most of us at some time in our lives, or maybe several times, have thought that we had found love, the real thing, only to find later that it wasn't what we thought it was. Like iron pyrites, there is nothing wrong with the feelings we might have experienced; it's just that there is a variety of emotions and thought processes that can and do arise and, if we are fooled by them, we will later endure disappointment and pain. Jealousy, rejection, hurt pride, resentment and anger are just some of the painful experiences that can result. We won't dwell on those here but it is important to be able to distinguish some of the more common versions of fool's gold. Even our painful experiences of the past can help us to find and develop the source of love within us. The trouble sometimes, though, is that the painful experiences provide so strong a memory that we then prevent ourselves from expressing love as fully as we might.

1. *Attachment – the biggest fake of all*

When we are drawn to something and do not want to let go of it, we are suffering from what is known as attachment. None of us is totally free from this state, which exists in many forms, not just in relationships, and gives rise to countless expressions, emotions, beliefs and thought processes. A person can become attached to people, to property, to ideals, to circumstances and so on. Sometimes we might come across someone who proclaims that he or she is attached to nothing at all; a little questioning usually reveals quite quickly that that is not the case. Attachment is both a mental and an emotional phenomenon. It is as though the mind extends tentacles or feelers into things, people or circumstances that it wants to acquire or retain. Attachment involves the mind sinking hooks into different concepts or pictures it has built up in an attempt to hold on to them. Obvious examples are the many forms of possessiveness or desire; but attachment can also be holding on to a state of affairs. People often resist change because they are unwittingly attached to the present and fear losing it rather than because the change is bad in itself.

Some attachments can be very apparent, such as in the case of an addiction; others – such as a desire to maintain control, for example – may be less obvious yet equally as strong. To unearth and release all our attachments is a lifetime's work; but as soon as we start the process, no matter at what point in life we are, we become easier with ourselves and happier. Wherever we are now is a starting point.[8]

This is important because no matter what form attachment takes, it results in mental constriction or tension. In

---

8 A lady once came to an introductory session on meditation I was leading and, although she had a good session, she said it was too late in life for her to begin making changes. It is never too late and, if we don't make changes now, when will we?

terms of energy, which governs our subtle responses, we are tighter and less able to love. The heart centre is sometimes described as a lotus, whose petals open as we express love more and more; those same petals shrink into a tight bud when we succumb to the strictures of attachment. Even if we take good care of our body and our appearance, if our heart is closed, we are not a complete human being. Rather like one of those fancy roses from the bargain florist that have been raised under glass but never open fully nor have any fragrance, everything might appear good from the outside but the inner quality is lacking in expression. Inside, mental and emotional tension results in a distorted view of the world and everyone in it.

Attachment most commonly becomes wrongly labelled as love in relationships, whether they be between family members, friends, lovers, spouses or otherwise. Attachment means that mentally and emotionally we are drawn towards and hold on to the other person. Often without realising it, we seek to fulfil our needs from the other person or from the relationship. That doesn't mean to say that our relationship is entirely selfish because often there is some give and take, although not always. There may be love present in the relationship but there is attachment too.

If the other person turns away from us or prefers another person over us and we feel rejected or perhaps feel some pang of jealousy, it is certain that some attachment is present in us. If we fear losing someone who is close to us, we are attached to them.

Letting go of attachment and simply loving – without complication, expectation or attachment – is key. This isn't easy; in fact it is extremely difficult to do it completely, but gradually, very gradually, we can work towards it. Each step sets us free a little more. The freedom that results isn't freedom from anything outside us, but freedom from our own mental creations. We created our own attachments and so have the power to dissolve them.

2. *Infatuation*

Infatuation isn't love but when we are in the throes of it, it isn't so easy to tell the difference. Others may see quite clearly that we are severely afflicted, but the deeply infatuated person will often have convinced themselves that they are in love. It is common for young people to suffer from infatuation more; their emotions are often less stable, as indeed are their hormones, than in someone more mature and most of us in younger days will have had a crush on someone at some point. It is infatuation that gives rise to fans of celebrities doing all sorts of things in the name of their idols that a clear mind would not contemplate. Serious cases can develop into obsession, resulting in bizarre and often harmful behaviour, but it is the milder forms of infatuation that are most often mistaken for love.

The infatuated person sees certain qualities in the other that are interpreted as desirable and so the other person becomes an object of desire. Whether those qualities are actually present is not important; it is the fact that they are perceived to be present that is material. Those same qualities may be perceived by others also but the infatuated person finds them particularly attractive and so feels drawn towards them very strongly. When these feelings are not reciprocated or acknowledged, they can be very painful. Without attempting to analyse infatuation or its causes in a clinical way, it is nevertheless helpful to understand that it is a mental and emotional state that arises from wanting something for oneself. Love, on the other hand, seeks nothing for itself.

3. *Falling in love – Romeo's glass jewel*

Few of us have not, at some time or another, fallen in love. Sometimes, we may come across someone who always seems to be falling into and out of relationships. They enjoy the buzz of the chemical changes in the body and the emotions that result from the excitement of a new relationship. Is that love? Almost certainly not. However, the process of attraction and its possible development into falling in love merits some attention because there is often a convincing manifestation of love that is in fact fool's gold.

When a person falls in love, certain biochemical changes occur. It is also true that *any* mental and emotional state alters the body's chemistry. Fear, ecstasy, anger and hilarity, for example, all create changes in the body.[9] But falling in love creates a change that lasts for some time. Emotionally, a

---

9 One of the earliest theories was the James-Lange theory which suggested that physiological changes cause emotions. However, the Cannon-Bard theory asserted that physiological changes occur simultaneously with emotions. The *fight or flight response* was a term coined by Walter Bradford Cannon for the biochemical reactions, such as increased adrenalin resulting in changes to breathing, blood pressure and heart rate, occurring when a person is under stress.

person falling in love is quite strong in some ways and can have the courage and determination to do things that normally wouldn't be contemplated. There can also be considerable vulnerability in the fear that one's love will be unrequited. Falling in love is a time of altered behaviour, altered perception and, usually, instability.

There is a subtle mental process unfolding throughout the period of falling in love and it begins with attraction. Attraction is caused by perception; there is something in the other person, some quality or qualities, we feel drawn to. If we look deeply enough, we may find that what we are drawn to is a feeling of wholeness or completeness that we believe the other person can bring to us. Turning that round a little bit, there is something at some level within us that we feel is missing – a gap or partial vacuum that the other person can fill or satisfy.

Sometimes we might hear someone say they are looking for, or have found, their "soulmate". It is possible, and indeed it happens, that there are connections, like streams or currents, that draw people together. That can happen in all sorts of ways and isn't necessarily confined to personal relationships. The term "soulmate" is something of a misnomer because in a true sense all members of the human race are soulmates to each other, which is why love, the subject of this book, is so extraordinarily important. There are, of course, different levels of attraction, the most superficial (but often the most motivating) being that of sex, which we will address shortly, and the deepest where two or more people serve a common, altruistic (and hence spiritual) purpose in an atmosphere of true love.

Falling in love can and does happen where there is a deeper underlying draw between two people, but it also frequently happens where there is not. Nevertheless, the emotional pull can feel just as strong in the latter case and it is not unusual for those experiencing it to believe that "this is it", that they have met the partner of their dreams and that being together will bring eternal happiness. The biochemical response will produce all sorts of changes that may often give the impression of radiance of the skin and a sparkle and depth to the eyes. People in love are like flowers coming into full bloom: subject to the right conditions and maturity there is a rapid ripening process going on and the hormones are lively.[10] No wonder we are unstable when subject to this!

The point to recognise in this process is that no matter how we dress it up, when we are falling in love we are seeking something for ourselves – the sense of increasing wholeness, perhaps, or the emotional and mental uplift of being with someone we admire. Love may, and often does, manifest *in addition* to what is going on, but the barb of Cupid's arrow can be painful because it is the product of desire, the working out (or not) of wish fulfilment. So we see gold but it isn't gold. Falling in love is like an adrenalin rush but true love has unending stamina of the kind that could run a marathon. Unlike attraction and desire, love is prepared to lose everything for the sake of another and does not seek to hold on.

---

10 E.g. raised levels of cortisol – as discussed in research by D. Marazziti and D. Canale, University of Pisa 2004 on the hormonal changes of people falling in love. See *Psychoneuroendocrinology*, 29/7 (August 2004), 931–936.

People will always fall in love, because it is human nature, but our purpose is to bring something extraordinary into life – the XYZ factor.

4. *Sex*

Sex is one of the strongest motivators and deepest desires within the human psyche, so it is important that we spend a few moments considering it in the context of love and its false indicators. Because sexual desire can arise within a loving relationship, it would be an oversimplification to say that sex has nothing to do with love; moreover it is possible for love to emerge in a relationship that begins as a predominantly sexual one. In either case, desire forms an important aspect of sex. Part of that stems from the purely biological side to sex – reproduction of the species. Our bodies are programmed for sexual reproduction and so desires can naturally arise from hormonal and other biochemical changes.

If we look a little more deeply at the organic function, we might also become aware that underlying and informing the body is a subtle energy system. Part of that system is better known as the network of meridians that are used in acupuncture and other healing arts, but the meridians are only part of the picture. In Tibetan medicine, the energies are described as "winds"[11], which gives a hint of how subtle, and indeed volatile, they are. At various levels of expression, subtle forms

---

11 See e.g. *Health Through Balance – Introduction to Tibetan Medicine,* Dr Yeshe Dhonden and Jeffrey Hopkins, Snow Lion Publications 1986; and *Tibetan Ayurveda,* Robert Sachs (Inner Traditions 2001).

of energy affect the body, its nervous system, its general functioning and our moods. Our emotional and mental states both affect the balance and flow of that energy and are affected by it. Different states of mind and emotions cause changes and if those are strong or prolonged, the flow of subtle energy can be altered or even obstructed to such an extent that the changes can become a semi-permanent condition. These can have physical effects resulting in health problems if the energy disturbance remains uncorrected. Sometimes we may see that a person has poor posture and, although we cannot know all the causes of it, usually there is an energy problem lying underneath which itself stems from something deeper.

The point about energy and sex is that very often there is a deep energy problem in and around what is sometimes called the sacral energy centre. This centre corresponds to part of the lower abdomen a little above the pubic area. If energy is too highly concentrated there, usually because of stagnation in the energy circulatory system, the individual will often experience a distorted sexual expression or unbalanced desire. When the sex drive is too high, unbalanced or distorted, feelings of attraction may run very high and so there is strong desire. (Of course, there can also be the opposite effect where stagnation or blockage of the body's subtle energy can cause a degree of frigidity.)

Strong desire can often be mistaken in the person experiencing it for love. The words "I want you" can so easily be turned into "I love you". The person saying them may even believe what they utter, as may the person hearing them. Either way, the eventual result can be painful because, whether the attraction to the other person is sexual or something else, such as money, security, status and so on, once the desire is sated and inevitably wanes, the relationship comes under strain and all too often breaks down with painful consequences.

LOVE IS INDISCRIMINATIVE – AND PAINLESS

Contrary to popular belief, true love does not mean pain. Love, real love, transcends everything, even death. To be able to express or experience love that is pure and free of attachment is natural, it is our heritage, but our conditioning is such that it has become difficult. Like sunshine, love should radiate from us throughout our environment. Sunshine does not discriminate; nor does love. Our minds, however, do discriminate and it is because of our discriminating minds that we find the expression of pure love so difficult.

Love purifies the person who loves, simply because love is pure. As we love, the body becomes stronger and the mind more flexible. With flexibility of mind, there is less stress and tension. No matter what date is on our birth certificate, love makes us younger and the world for us a better place. The world becomes a better place for everyone else, too, as a loving heart makes a better human being and better human beings create a better society. Without trying to analyse any causes as to why we cannot at the moment radiate love completely throughout our environment, it is a healthy thing to reflect that our potential is in fact to do just that and have the intention that, no matter how long a road that may appear to be, step by step we will do so.

3

WATER, FIRE AND PASSION { UNCONDITIONAL LOVE AND OTHER MISUNDERSTANDINGS

LOVE IS SIMPLY THAT

People talk and write about unconditional love as though it were something superior; but love *is* unconditional and cannot be anything else. Love needs for itself only the opportunity for expression. But if there is no need to describe love as unconditional, is there such a thing as *conditional* love?

It really is important to understand what is going on within ourselves because if we label a feeling as love when it isn't, we or someone else is likely to suffer later on. But just as importantly, if we label something as not being love when in fact it is, we may miss out on strengthening a very good quality within us.

Each and every one of us has love within us. The extent to which it is felt and expressed depends on a number of factors but they could all be summarised in the word *consciousness*. Our state of consciousness varies from moment to moment and is coloured by our emotions, our thought patterns, the state of our body and nervous system and so on. So far as the expression of love is concerned, our consciousness is rather like a tap. Sometimes our love may be a dribble and at other times it may gush forth; at other times still, it may be turned off. What some people say is that if the tap closes, the love that was expressed before the tap closed was conditional and so was either of poor quality or wasn't love at all. But just as water doesn't cease to be water merely because it isn't coming out of the tap, love still is; it just needs the tap to be opened. Let us be clear about this: love is love.

Love is the most natural expression of a human being. When the mind is uncluttered, open and clear and the emotions are settled, it is natural to love. Love may emerge in different ways but in essence it arises as understanding, tenderness and a feeling of oneness or unity with what is loved. It may be felt towards an animal, a plant, towards nature in general and certainly towards other human beings, although our perception of other humans can sometimes cloud the mind. If we go to help someone who is in distress without having to think about it, we can understand that there is a spontaneous reaction or response of caring; in the same sort of way, love is a spontaneous response in the heart to something or someone we see or have in mind. Automatically, the tap is open and love flows forth.

IMPURE LOVE?

Feelings towards our fellow human beings can be extraordinarily complex, particularly with those who are close to us. Some would say that love is sometimes impure because of the complexity of feelings. But isn't that merely another way of saying that there are two types of love – pure and impure – instead of unconditional and conditional? The important thing to grasp is that all love is good. Other emotions may arise that make relationships difficult at times but if we express love, we are allowing an amazing universal energy and quality to flow through us.

Consider a glass of water that is full of mud, bacteria and so on. Is the water impure or is the water still water? If the mud and bacteria are removed by filtration, the water itself is not any different. The impurities have simply been removed. There is no less water; it is just as wet and able to hydrate. To make our garden beautiful, we need to ensure that our plants have sufficient water but it doesn't especially matter to them whether the water is clean or whether it has bits of dirt in it.

If we think of pure love as being without all the bits and pieces, we would be thinking of a love that was rather like distilled water, with all the essence driven out of it. Water that is good for us humans to drink is full of minerals and trace elements that are essential to life. Love does not need to be devoid of all human emotion. True, love in its essence is selfless but all of us have degrees of selfishness in our make-up and so our love will be coloured by our personality.[12]

Love needs feelings for true expression. The idealist may say that we should be dispassionate and that is true to an extent in that the mind is often muddied by emotion. We should be aiming for a clear mind as that is part of the process of enlightenment. But we all experience emotions and the level of dispassion we need is not one which is out of touch with our feelings. What is needed is a mind that is clear enough to recognise emotions that are present and yet operate clearly in spite of them. To love fully is to love with one's whole being and that means we have to engage our feelings. We cannot have a full heart without feeling, yet many think we should only engage the mind. Such thinking leads to a heart that is like a dried prune – the sweetness is inherent but needs releasing through the application of moisture.

If we classify love as unconditional and analyse whether we are marring our love by experiencing emotions, we run a real risk of making ourselves prematurely dispassionate. That is like turning the tap off when the water needs

---

12 There is a tendency for many people who follow what might be described as new-age thinking to idealise what the world should be like. One of the dangers with that type of thinking is that it is possible to detach oneself from most of humanity which is struggling in the grist of daily life. Walking round in a self-created insulated bubble, it is so easy to declare an unconditional love for all mankind. Whilst that would be marvellous if it were true, what generally happens is that there is an *intellectual* recognition that such love would be an ideal state and the ego does a fairly good job of building up a belief that that state has been achieved.

to flow. The result, so often, is a degree of aloofness that manifests in indifference and that, no matter how good the intention, is a poison to the growth of the heart and to consciousness.

WHICH IS BETTER – LOVE OR KNOWLEDGE?

There is a tendency in some people who have very good intentions to categorise things into pigeonholes. It is almost as though they have a set of boxes to tick and once something is ticked they feel there is nothing more to be done. For example, they may well have read and intellectually understood that spiritual enlightenment has two major aspects – compassion and wisdom. All that needs to be done, they think, is to acquire those two qualities, tick the boxes and they're done. Enlightenment achieved. Then they find that life still isn't quite as fulfilling as it might be and so they look for another system of knowledge – another teacher, perhaps, or another group or some more books. More boxes to tick. This sort of thing happens in many areas of life, and can be spotted when someone begins a new interest – t'ai chi, for example – with great enthusiasm but does not have the patience to deepen their practice. They learn the rudiments of one move and then go on to the next. Box ticked. Having learnt the rudiments of all the moves (if indeed they progress that far), they think all their boxes are ticked and they are done. They then read about chi, the vital energy, and ask questions about it, wanting to absorb more and more knowledge, but their actual practice and experience remain at a superficial level.

So many people are hungry for knowledge that they go round trying to suck it up like vacuum cleaners and all the titbits of knowledge they pick up are swept into the dust bag, and there they remain. If knowledge changes us or others for the better or makes the world a better place, who can argue that it is wrong? But if knowledge isn't useful, the only point to it is to exercise the brain cells or help us to answer quiz questions. Wise teachers have traditionally refused to answer deeply esoteric questions from their students not because the knowledge was harmful but to stop the students from cluttering up their minds with information that served no purpose. In today's society, people absorb so much information from newspapers, magazines, television and the internet. How much of that information is useful or raises awareness? The answer has to be *very little*.

So although some knowledge is necessary for enlightenment, too much of it becomes a hindrance. Development of the heart centre and of the qualities of the heart actually has nothing to do with knowledge at all. It is an expansion of consciousness and a very special expansion of consciousness at that. Intellectual understanding is only useful if it helps to break down some of the beliefs within us that are preventing that expansion; after that, it can often get in the way. Perhaps it is the conditioning created by an education requiring the assimilation of a million and one facts that is responsible for the belief that more and more knowledge is the way to find ourselves; but many who thirst for knowledge as a collection of facts are doing a very good job of avoiding themselves.

Whilst looking for knowledge "out there", they are successfully keeping their focus and awareness away from their own nature. Yet it is only within our own nature that true knowledge can be found.

A lovely story of the Buddha describes how he was addressing an assembly and simply held up a flower. Almost all who were present were trying to work out what the significance of the flower was. They were applying their intellects to what was being offered to them and so missed the point entirely. One, however, had a broad grin on his face because he simply connected with the Buddha and his unspoken teaching *at a deeper level of consciousness or awareness.* He experienced a knowing that is far beyond the intellect and that cannot be expressed in words.

Knowledge without love has been said to be like a lot of dry bones. Love is the most important thing in the world because it brings and holds together. Love raises the level of consciousness like nothing else but because it cannot be described easily, it runs second to knowledge and indeed to money and material things in the popularity stakes. Love is not something we can tick a box for. It is the expression of our true nature; it is the innermost of the innermost, the realisation and flowering of the most sacred part of our being.

SO PASSION CAN BE GOOD

Everything, according to ancient Indian philosophy, has three qualities or *gunas* and everything in the universe arises from the play of these three *gunas*. The first of these is called *tamas* and can broadly be described as expressing the qualities of inertia and solidity; the second, *rajas*, manifests as activity and stimulation, and the third is *sattva* – consistency, balance or harmony. None of these three is innately right or wrong because each is needed, but they need to remain in correct proportion to each other. For example, the body needs a certain amount of inertia for its solidity and structure, it needs metabolism and action to maintain warmth and health and it needs the balancing effect of homoeostasis to maintain order. On the other hand, too much *tamas* (inertia) will produce lethargy, dullness and possibly too much body weight; and an excess of *rajas* will generate too much heat, stimulation and excitation. *Tamas* (inertia) is overcome, and therefore balanced, by *rajas* (activity) and *rajas* is balanced by *sattva* (harmony). There are similar, albeit not identical, concepts in Chinese philosophy with the need to balance *kan* and *li* (water and fire) and *yin* and *yang* (negative and positive).

The principle of the *gunas* applies to mental states also. For example, if the mind is dull and we simply can't be bothered with anything, the quality of *tamas* or inertia is said to be predominant. To overcome that dullness, some stimulation – *rajas* – is needed. Once the mind is sufficiently stimulated and alert, rather than giving it further stimulation, it is better for there to be some wholesome and balancing mental activity, something that is harmonious, applying the quality of *sattva*. But until the waking-up process is complete and all dullness has been dissipated, something that is soothing and calming is not going to be particularly productive. If we are sleepy, for instance, meditation is not going to be helpful even though meditation is an excellent thing for the mind when we are fully awake. Although a clear, pure and harmonious mental state may seem the ideal to aim for, it is only ideal and attainable if and when the mind is sufficiently ripe. In our quest for uncovering the full potential for love within us, it is not sufficient simply to decide to love, to imagine we love or to recite an affirmation of love. Those can be useful adjuncts but by themselves they are mainly actions of the intellect. So much wrong thinking arises from missing the vital point: that until the mind is ripe and ready for the next stage, the next stage just won't work, let alone various stages further forward. Development of the heart is a ripening process and so we need to apply what the head and the heart are ready for and not go leaping too far ahead. Applying the principle of the three *gunas*, most of us still have a considerable amount of mental *tamas* or inertia that needs to be overcome. Of course we also have mental *rajas* because the minds of the vast majority of human beings are overactive but not all of that over-activity is particularly helpful; in fact it can be simply exhausting. In our theme of developing love, there is a mental *rajas* that invokes the emotions in a positive way and that is to become passionate about love.

Being passionate about love doesn't mean being hot headed and it certainly isn't a reference to the animal passion of sex. But there does need to be a certain fire or heat to melt the indifference (which is a form of mental inertia) that exists to some degree in the ordinary human heart. When we see another human being, there should be a surge of warmth, a feeling of very strong connection with the other person, whether we know them or not. For many of us that either doesn't happen or it only happens in respect of people we know and like well. To have warm feelings towards *all* people we come across is a difficult standard to achieve but it is possible and is what we are eventually aiming for in opening the heart centre. These feelings are not the artificial and shallow gushings of a theatrical "lovey" or socialite but something very deep and potentially very powerful. This energy, once we can harness it and bring it forth, is transforming. It can change us, turning us into much stronger spiritual beings, who can uplift others, literally raising their spirits. For this we need to be in touch with our emotions. We need to be able to feel our feelings and not have any measure of aloofness. Most of us tend to become excited about the wrong things and are too often anaesthetised against the things that really matter.

The heart centre or chakra is often depicted symbolically as a flower. This is a very helpful representation because, just like a flower, it develops in various stages until it becomes fully open. In most of us, the heart centre could be likened to a tightly closed bud which is perhaps showing just a hint of colour between the sepals. Gradually, given the right conditions of light, warmth and moisture, the bud will show more and more colour and eventually blossom into a gorgeous bloom. In this analogy, we could say that the needed light is understanding, the warmth is love and the moisture is feeling. A bud needs all three conditions whether it is a flower or our heart. Our hearts cannot develop without some understanding because ignorance is like darkness; we cannot see things as they really are when we are immersed in ignorant beliefs. Warmth and moisture go together because feelings that are cold are like death. Feelings need love, they need warmth to nurture life. And warmth without moisture is like dry heat in a desert; we may become fiery but we also become brittle in the heat.

One thing we can address is that in today's society, too many of us have become accountants. Whilst real accountants provide an essential function, it seems as if today there is a large majority of people who are overly concerned with the cost of things, whether that cost is measured in terms of time, money or energy. There is a prevailing attitude that prevents many members of our society from doing anything unless there appears some measurable return. Life seems to be dominated by a desire to make money or to save money or perhaps to earn recognition or to have this or that. When we are like that, it often requires a crisis to change us – something that shakes us to our dry bones.[13] But we shouldn't have to wait for a crisis; we simply have to change now.

LOVER, LOVE AND BELOVED

Consider this for a moment – is there a need for a beloved? The word *beloved* isn't used here to indicate a personal

---

13 Crises let in some "moisture" because all of a sudden different values apply in life when we are shaken and the comfortable stability of our existence is threatened.

relationship, necessarily. The word itself might conjure up thoughts of lovers in the personal sense or perhaps for some it will bring to mind spiritual devotion. However, what I would like us to do now is to consider the use of the word in the context of *that which is loved*. If we look at it this way and think for a moment, we will perhaps begin to realise that we cannot love nothing.

Whatever activity is undertaken, there has to be a doer, there has to be the action itself and there has to be an object or thing in respect of which activity is done. As you read this, for example, there is you, the reader, there is the text and there is the act of reading. If you put the book down or even close the eyes or avert your sight, both you and the text still exist but there is no act of reading linking the two. Similarly when we know or experience something, there is (a) the knower or the one who experiences, (b) the process of knowing and (c) the object – that which is known. We cannot know inside a vacuum nor can we act or experience inside a vacuum. All the time we are awake, we are both a knower and an experiencer. That means we are always doing something and always have awareness of something. You are aware of these words but will also be having thought processes going on whilst you are reading them. Even thinking has a threefold expression of thinker, mental processes or thoughts and the objects of the thoughts, i.e. what we are thinking about. You and I are constant doers, knowers and experiencers.

This is significant in developing love because in order to broaden and deepen this wonderful quality, it is necessary to have an object of love. The lover requires something or someone to love because, without that, there can be no love and therefore no lover either. In order to exist, love needs the threefold expression of (1) the actor, knower or experiencer, (2) the process of loving and (3) that which is loved. Not only can we not love at all without this magical threesome, if we want to deepen our expression of love, we have to change ourselves and our perceptions because although we need the object of love in order to love, that object itself may not change. The lover needs to change the way he or she interprets what is perceived through the senses and through the mind, otherwise the process of loving will remain the same.

The purpose of making this point now is that the unfolding of love in our hearts is something very real. If we simply live in a remote and peaceful place imagining that we love all and sundry, any love that we conjure up will be very weak. Or even if we simply close the door on our busy world, retire to a quiet room and have pleasant thoughts about people, that is only going to achieve so much. In the same way that physical fitness will not be achieved by sitting in a chair or lying in bed visualising exercises or even watching a fitness programme, simply imagining that we love is not enough. It is so easy to be an idealist but it is not enough. It is essential that we apply love in our daily lives where all manner of things will crop up and challenge us. Yes, it's much harder, but it's the only way we are going to make our love real and lasting.

4

DOWN TO BUSINESS

LOVE IS POSSIBLE AT EVERY LEVEL

Few people would argue that our society is not fast, often impersonal and driven largely by economic and market forces. Commerce leaves its imprint everywhere but, like it or loathe it, the world as we know it could not operate without it. The public perception of many organisations is that they are too big, too remote and only present a friendly face (if they do so at all) when they are after something – usually our money. Strangers, too, may appear unfriendly and remote to us although that is probably more of an appearance than a fact. Nevertheless, we may not feel that our modern society is particularly nurturing or loving. Almost daily, instances are reported of people appointed to responsible positions lining their pockets to the detriment of those they serve. Even our healthcare systems are forced to abide by key performance indicators and statistics rather than being fountains of human kindness focusing on the healing arts which, one might be forgiven for thinking, is their core purpose. It appears that our modern world is driven largely by money and its accumulation.

However, as any society is merely a collection of individuals and reflects the collective consciousness of those who make it up, each of us has a responsibility towards the condition of our society as it is now. And as each of us has enormous capacity for love, it must be possible for love to be expressed in society and its activities; indeed, even a global expression of love must be possible. This may seem an enormous presumption and one that, even if it is theoretically possible, has the sound of a romantic pipe dream. But air travel, space exploration, computer technology and all manner of things we take for granted today were pipe dreams at one time. What will be useful for us to do in this chapter is to look at some examples of where, often in spite of appearances, love has a firm place in society, with potential to flourish in many different ways. If we can see and acknowledge that, we should be able to envisage something far greater, something that each of us can and must play a very real and practical part in. The foundation for any society is the human beings who make it up, and so let's start with the home.

LOVE IN THE HOME

It is so fundamentally important to the spiritual, mental and emotional well-being, as well as the physical health, of the human race that each and every home is filled with love. It doesn't matter if we live on our own or in a household of many. If love is absent, the home is not a healthy one. Although that is obvious, or should be, it may not be at the forefront of most people's minds that the *greater* the love there is in a home, the healthier it will be for everyone within it. This love isn't something that is reserved for our nearest and dearest; it is love for the whole of one's home environment. Please do not confuse this with attachment to the home; that is something different and we looked at attachment in general terms in chapter 2. If there is love for the home, there is a deep respect for it and for everyone who steps into it. The home should be a place of sanctity and a refuge from the bustle of the outside world. We should feel blessed as soon as we enter and we should bless the house also – not in the form of words necessarily but simply from a level of feeling, which may be a mixture of gratitude and an intention of goodness. By doing so we immediately uplift our surroundings and at some level everyone who enters the home receives a positive effect from the general energy of the place. Whether we live in a grand house with beautiful gardens or in an apartment or bedsit is immaterial. The important thing is to create a pleasant, supportive environment or build on the one that is already present.

Within the home we should smile and go about our activity easily. If we do everything with haste or a misplaced sense of urgency, we cannot fill what we do with the wonderful heart-energy we all possess. Nearly every home has clutter somewhere and we should take steps to de-clutter on a frequent basis. Where there is clutter, there is stagnation and untidiness which reflects on, and impinges upon, our mental state. For love to fill the immediate world of our home, the place where we live and rest our head at night, it should be entirely free of negative influences; happy and peaceful and filled with joy. For some people that might seem a tall order, particularly if other members of the household are noisy, untidy and don't share a similar view. It might seem impossible also if we are troubled by neighbours who are difficult. Nevertheless, if our intention is good we will have considerable impact on the energy of the home in spite of difficulties.

Our home in many ways creates a basis for our everyday consciousness. If the atmosphere in the home is unsettled, so are we. If it is happy and bright, then we are too. Whatever we do outside, whether it is work, study, caring for someone, running errands or recreation, our consciousness in that activity is deeply affected by the atmosphere we have created in the home. Do we welcome visitors warmly or are we guarded and insular? If we have created a mental moat around us, it will be reflected in how we react to the world and others will not receive the wonderful warmth we are capable of giving out. On the other hand, if we invite guests with the ulterior motive that they will think well of us, our acquisitive and proud nature will taint what we do in our daily life.

If every home on our planet were filled with warmth, joy and happiness, if every single dwelling radiated love and generosity of spirit, wouldn't the world be an amazing place? Just one happy home affects the environment, and many can completely transform it. We might think that our home is already filled with joy and there is nothing further to be done. But every one of us can further enrich our surroundings because we are all capable of greater love. There is no end point, no stage at which we can say, "That's it," because life isn't like that; it never stops evolving and neither will your heart or mine.

TRANSFORMING THE WORKPLACE

I remember going to a motivational seminar many years ago and the speaker asked the audience if they loved their work. That question made me think because although I loved the people I worked with, I couldn't put my hand on my heart and say that there was love for all the work I did. Later, that position changed. The work itself didn't change a great deal but my feelings and attitude towards it did because I came to realise that part of me had been missing from what I was doing. Probably the speaker used the word "love" in the context of being enthusiastic and thoroughly enjoying work. That doesn't matter. If we love what we are doing we will be enthusiastic but what I would like us to do for a few moments is to think about love and the workplace in a deeper way. If you don't go to work in the conventional sense, this still applies to your everyday activity, so please read on.

Everyone has the right and the capacity to be happy in their work. It may be that our work puts us under great pressure or it may be very mundane; it may require us to interact with people who are not happy and can be very unpleasant. However, our true nature is boundless and the more we become aware of, and in touch with, our boundless nature, the greater our ability to deal with any situation with equanimity. When we love, our wonderful nature is manifesting itself; and so to be able to deal with all our daily activity in an unruffled and happy state, we need to undertake everything we do with an attitude of loving kindness.

If you have just picked this book up and opened it at this point without having read and digested the earlier parts, you could be forgiven for thinking that the possibility of transforming where we work through the application of love is an ideal that is out of touch with reality. But if you have grasped that the process involves changing ourselves, unleashing our inner potential and changing the very atmosphere around us, you might more easily accept that each of us has an extraordinary ability to change our environment. We can change it for the worse or for the better simply by how we are. The wonderful thing is you don't have to take my word, or anyone else's, for it; indeed, everything in this book is presented for those who read it to apply or not apply as they wish. Of course, many who read this will already apply a good many of the principles and fill their places of employment or businesses with positivity and understanding. If that is the case with you, you will want to build on what you do now.

A barrier to love in any environment (and we shall look at obstacles more in the next chapter) is that human beings have an extraordinary tendency to be selfish – and if we work only for the money or status it provides us with, we can be sure we are ripe for improvement! So the starting point for most of us is to regard the needs of others as being at least as important as our own. This is not to become a doormat but to put things in a more enlightened perspective. If we already do this, that's good; otherwise it's something to work on. Either way, one of the tricks for retraining our attitude towards others is to see them differently. Instead of seeing the people we work with or have dealings with impersonally, we can imagine that we have known them for a very long time, to the extent that there is a deep underlying closeness that is not openly manifested but is very real. This positive use of the imagination can have extraordinary effects on our consciousness. Imagine that the people you work with, no matter whether you like them or not, find them obnoxious or don't even give them a second thought, are your very close spiritual friends. We can picture this friendship as going back a very long time, to before we were born. (There is a much wider acceptance today of the continuity of consciousness and the role of birth, life, death and subsequent rebirth as part of the evolutionary process of consciousness. If you are comfortable with that, you will find this relatively easy to grasp and, if not, you can nevertheless imagine an acquaintanceship that goes back a very long way.)

This is, of course, a very private matter because what we are trying to do with this approach is change both the way we view others and how we feel about them.[14] This is, in fact, a very old method and the Buddhist Mahayana tradition, for example, advocates viewing the other person as having been our mother or father in a previous life as an excellent way of generating loving kindness. Not everyone

---

14 How they feel about and view us is their affair and we mustn't confuse, and probably alarm, others by talking about this. That is important.

in our western culture is comfortable with that concept, though, often because of unhappy memories and so we should do what we are comfortable and happy with.

This practice, incidentally, is not one to be restricted to the workplace. Learning to love others or to love them more by viewing them differently is very important in our development. It is also extraordinarily powerful and effective. At times we may feel a little emotional but that does no harm unless we take it too far. It means that the blocks within us are melting. However, just as ice will thaw in the sunshine only to freeze again when the sun disappears, we need to keep practising the technique and not simply regard it as a novelty to be completed just a few times.

Loving the work that we do can be more difficult, particularly if we answer to those whose ideas on what we should be doing do not conform to our own. Similarly, it may be difficult to love what we do if it is very mundane, repetitive or emotionally stressful. Whatever the nature of our work, we should try our best to love it. We can begin to do that by taking a pride in what we do (but not becoming attached to it, which can lead to personal pride) and doing it with care. Whatever we touch is affected by how we are. If we resent what we are doing, we inject a little bit of negativity into it. That has an immediate effect on our own energy system and we also pass that negative energy to others. Happily, the opposite is true and our aim as spiritual beings (which we all are) should be to fill everything with goodness.

In a nutshell, then, we have the potential to transform our workplace by changing our view of others and by caring, really caring, about what we do. The workplace is, after all, a small unit in society and society can only change for the better if all the units within it change. As we each become a little more enlightened, a little kinder and more compassionate, our planet gradually becomes a better place; and that, believe me, is just what love is trying to do.

DOES LOVE HAVE ANY BUSINESS IN BUSINESS?

Except for a tiny minority run on philanthropic lines, most commercial enterprises are run for the main purpose of making money. Whether it is for profit or not, though, almost every business provides a service of some sort. A whole book could be devoted to the service aspect of business and its potential for contributing to human growth and evolution. In spite of that, in modern times there have been many examples of greed in business and its devastating effects, sometimes on a huge scale, have disgusted fair-minded people everywhere. Sadly, that has created a spin-off of increasing levels of cynicism in ordinary folk to what is in fact a necessary part of the modern world. Unless we become recluses or can manage total self-sufficiency (which actually requires money in the first place) we cannot avoid the products and services of commerce nor, unless all our affairs are dealt with for us, can we avoid dealing with businesses of different sorts on an almost daily basis. We have to pay for the energy that lights and heats our homes, for our clothes, food and so on. Most of us have to pay taxes of various sorts for the provision of an enormous variety of services to our communities, both nationally and locally. A list, if we made one, of our connections with business would go on and on, even if our lifestyle is a simple one.

At its core, any business is in essence a means of interaction between a person or group of persons we could call A and another person or persons we could call B whereby something is exchanged for something else. A provides B with X in exchange for Y. So a business is a means for transactions to take place between people and when we think of it in those simple terms, it isn't so difficult to see that love – of the unemotional kind – could have a very natural place in it. Any interaction between human beings can, and perhaps should, involve the heart in addition to the head. For many businessmen or businesswomen this may sound absurd and it is true that sometimes in business tough decisions have to be made. On the other hand, don't we need to have regard to the purpose of life? Whether a person is a magnate of a commercial empire or runs a corner shop, he or she is a spiritual being with a spiritual purpose. That purpose is different for everyone because we are all at varying stages of evolution but for no-one should love ever be excluded from the path.

How can love come into business, then? The first step has to be that whatever we do must be ethical. In other words, whatever we engage in and however we engage in it has to be from the standpoint, at the very least, that it causes no harm to others, not just physically but mentally and emotionally as well. More than that, a business should be conducted in such a way that it enhances life for others and in some small way makes this a better world. If a business is ethically driven, that is what it will do and, if we are in business, that should be our intention.

Many commercial interests might be difficult to classify as being ethical in purpose because the use of the products or services fulfils desires or demands that are not life-enhancing in effect. A tobacconist, for example, sells products that are not conducive, and are often harmful, to health. But the tobacconist probably started the business or perhaps inherited it as a way to provide for his or her family. The same reason applies to many other types of trade – the trade itself is not life-enhancing but was created out of necessity to make a living. Is it possible for love to have a place in such a trade? The answer must be "yes" because whenever we engage with another person, there is an opportunity for love to be felt in the heart. This may be mild at first, experienced as clarity and expressed in genuine fairness and friendliness or as goodwill. If we continually express goodwill, eventually love will come to the heart. Over time, the attitude towards the business may change and our work may become more fulfilling. If the original intention was to make a great deal of money and retire on the proceeds, that intention will almost certainly change. What love will not countenance is the exploitation of another human being. To become rich at another's expense is to set up causes for future suffering. We cannot be happy if we exploit – but we can be enormously happy if we love.

Business and spiritual growth are not incompatible. Better still, love *does* have a place in business and will show in fairness and kindness towards suppliers, customers and workforce. If we conduct our business with the desire for the highest good for all concerned in it or affected by it, and if we carry out our trade with kindness, the world will be all the richer. It is not a question of letting the heart rule the head but rather of allowing the heart to *guide* the head. There is never a time when love is irrelevant – and there is always plenty of scope for improvement! And although many people who read this may think none of it applies to them because they are not in business, please remember that all of us engage with businesses in one way or another and so the same principles apply. Be kind, honest and fair in your dealings with others, whether they be a vast energy-supply company, the post office where you buy your stamps or the corner shop. In short, whenever we pay for goods or services we are at that moment in business. It is entirely up to us whether we act with goodwill and kindness towards others but if we listen to our heart, we will know which is the right way to act and to be.

LOVE'S PLACE IN SOCIAL ACTIVITIES

By and large, humans are gregarious in nature. There are those who prefer to be alone but even for them there is inevitably a need for social contact at some point; very few people are true recluses. People are often drawn together by common interests, desires or needs. It makes sense, too, for people to organise themselves into groups because the effectiveness of a group is almost always far greater than the sum total of the individual members. Resources can be amassed and shared as can knowledge and experience. For the purpose of achieving an aim, a group of like minds is generally good and provides many opportunities for social intercourse. But the question for us in our theme is, does belonging to a social group (and this applies equally to an informal group, such as a circle of friends) provide an opportunity for the development of love, for opening the heart?

As this is a book on love and as love arises from selflessness, it is always worth looking at the true purpose of a group – is its nature driven by selfish motives or selfless ones? Very few groups indeed are totally selfless. Even those social groups that describe themselves as "service clubs", for example, are often self-serving in the main, most being vehicles for social gatherings foremost and any service to the community being secondary. There are organisations, too, whose main purpose is to serve their own members, such as a society, a sports club and so on. The formal objects of many clubs and societies can appear philanthropic on paper but all such groups are inevitably subject to human failings which often taint an otherwise apparently altruistic purpose. This is not a criticism of any group, just a statement of fact, and even many groups formed for spiritual reasons can be subject to this. If we belong to a group, it can be very helpful to examine *our own* motives for being a member. If we do that honestly, we will almost certainly find that there are some reasons that can be described as "doing it for me"; enjoyment, self-advancement, and recognition as well as seeking social support and interaction are all common possibilities. There is absolutely nothing wrong with those reasons but if we want to develop our own heart qualities, we need to be aware that they are there.

Love arises when selfish motives are set to one side and are replaced by genuine kindness that seeks nothing for itself. Love will flourish when there is a deep and lasting respect for our fellow group members. If, for example, we have joined a group or a class in order to acquire knowledge or skills, love will grow more readily if we have a deep respect for the teaching that we seek, for our fellow learners and for those who are doing their best to teach us. On the other hand, if we are not bothered about the other members of the group and want to take whatever is on offer to serve our own ends, our time is not going to be particularly joyful. Our mind is likely to be tarnished by negative thinking when things are not going the way we think they should. In short, we will have high expectations that will inevitably lead to disappointment and, instead of a heart that is juicy with the sweet elixir of life, we will have one that is like a dried-up prune or a sour grape.

The purpose of love in any group is to bring in the light of understanding, to bring a little of the divine into human activities. Sometimes we may find that the whole ethos of a group militates against that. If we find ourselves in such a group or wake up to the fact that a group we are in is retarding our inner spiritual growth because of negative tendencies within it, we have a responsibility to ourselves to do something about it – and in essence we have two choices. One is to continue our membership but nevertheless inwardly work on eliminating all obstructions to love within us. The other option is to consider whether we should remain a part of the group or can safely withdraw from it. What is not acceptable in spiritual terms is to take part in or be associated with negativity. The mental and emotional atmosphere of such groups is as conducive to spiritual well-being as being in a smoke-filled room is to health and vitality.

In time, groups in which love can flourish will themselves flourish; many of those that are predominantly selfish in nature and purpose will lose strength and eventually dissolve. What is important to understand, is that social and other groups are a necessary part of human expression and experience. To eschew groups is wrong; to discriminate wisely in choosing what we belong to is vital.

THE CONNECTION BETWEEN LOVE AND THE CARING PROFESSIONS

Although there have been physicians, healers and carers in one guise or another throughout human history, the welfare of society as a whole is a comparatively recent phenomenon. It is only over the last 200 years or so that western nations have developed, with varying degrees of success, welfare systems that began with schemes to aid the poor into sometimes quite sophisticated health and social security systems. Some would argue that those systems do not meet their intended aims, at least not in all countries, but it is better to have something than nothing, which unfortunately is what many poorer countries have.

Nursing and the various branches of the medical and caring professions are where one might expect loving kindness to find a ready outlet for expression. To be engaged in such work is an extraordinary privilege but is also extraordinarily hard, often involving much personal sacrifice. Society owes a great debt to those who spend much of their lives caring for others. But society is also performing a great disservice because in many countries love is not allowed to play a role in the healing and caring arts, having been replaced, so it seems, by performance targets, cost-cutting, fear of litigation and the like. Because love and loving kindness are the strongest healers, it is vital that we as a society begin to see health and caring in a new light.

Sadly, we live in a culture where blaming others has become an art form. Look at almost any newspaper and you will find it filled with judgemental statements about how other people are carrying out their various roles in life, be it their profession, livelihood or their private lives. To blame and judge is one of the major defence mechanisms of the ego. We could rightly say that in spiritual terms this is ugly and a complete anathema to love. It has no place in the heart of a person who seeks to love selflessly, to draw on their inner source and to lead a life filled with abundance; unfortunately, the tendency to judge and blame others is in most of us at least to some degree. Yet we expect our doctors, nurses, carers and specialists somehow to be perfect. How can we do that when as a society or a community we do not support them but instead take what we can from them and cast aspersions and incriminations when things go wrong? Some go further and start litigation, justifiably perhaps when there is a genuine need for compensation that is being denied. But the end result is that the caring services work within a poor atmosphere, where suspicion and fear are often present. It is difficult for love and healing to flourish in such an environment. Nobody is to blame except society itself and there isn't a magic formula except for there to be a complete change in attitude. That requires a change in collective consciousness; fortunately we can play a significant part in that by changing our own.

Healing and caring are divine in nature and spring from the heart of love and compassion. It goes without saying that the greater the love and compassion, the more effective the healing and caring will be. If we want the services in our communities to be effective and successful, we should remember the source of all welfare, which is universal. As such it is helpful to recognise that our hospitals, health centres, care homes and other outer expressions of healing within our communities are in effect a manifestation of the divine nature, albeit greatly imperfect due to the collective ignorance of mankind. If we want loving kindness to flourish within these centres of care and healing, which is a natural thing to desire and to occur, then we have to love and support those who provide the services. Imagine, for a moment, being a child again. If you are watched by someone who is waiting for you to make a mistake and to criticise you, what is it like? The atmosphere isn't happy, is it? Not only that, the chances of things going wrong are significantly increased when there is an expectation that they will. On the other hand, if we are told when things are going right, our actions tend to be better and contain fewer mistakes.

In essence, as a society *we* need to develop love and respect for those in these much criticised professions as much as *they* need to express (as many of them do) love and respect for those in their charge. Each of us has our part to play in this. You might say that surely this principle should apply to every service in our communities, not just health and care, and you would be absolutely right. But if we cannot get this part of community life right, what can we?

WISE GOVERNMENT – IS IT POSSIBLE?

If we can visualise something, it is possible, so it is said. The world of government and politics seems a universe away from any idea of wisdom, love and compassion. But a government reflects to a huge degree the consciousness of the people it represents. If the national collective consciousness is weak, the government will reflect that and then it is all too easy for selfish interests, corruption and greed to take a grip. The leadership of such a government will either look to prolonging its political life and position of power or it will be indecisive and lack assertiveness in its conduct. Similarly, if the will of the people is not behind it, the government will fear making decisions that require strength of character. Following the vein we have already touched on, we need to resist the very strong temptation to blame politicians, political parties and government leaders for the messes they seem to get us into. It is just too easy to say "it's their fault" or "politicians are all the same". If we do that, it means we do not have the eye of understanding and haven't looked deeply enough at the *real* underlying causes.

If we want a government to possess strength and wisdom (which are both aspects of love in its true sense), society itself has to change. There has to be a deep desire within the heart of society to express a living, loving kindness in the everyday organisation and operation of our communities. Only as collective consciousness begins to change will we see a major change in the way governments think and operate. This may seem a long way off, but it isn't impossible. Most people can identify many things that are wrong with our society's values; some blame parents, some blame education and many blame the government of the day. But that's to go back to a blame culture, which achieves nothing. If the values in society are wrong, only a will to change within individuals can put it right. Nor is it helpful to hark back to "the good old days"; we have to deal with today and, after all, the old days gave birth to current times.

There is much we can learn from other cultures and a look at the kingdom of Bhutan, the Land of the Thunder Dragon, nestling in the Himalayas, is very instructive and inspiring. Bhutan is famous for its governing theory, created by the previous king, that Gross National Happiness is far more important than Gross National Product.[15] Although the Bhutanese are embracing modern times, traditional values that maintain a strong culture; deep respect for one another;

---

15 There are many books and sources of further information on this. See, for example, *Blessings of Bhutan*, Ross and Blyth Carpenter, Hawaii University Press 2002.

and a lifestyle that promotes happiness are evident everywhere and that is the way the country is governed. The people of Bhutan may not have attained perfection but are living proof that a society based on happiness rather than personal profit *is* possible. Not only is it possible, should such an environment not be the aim of all of us? If we can imagine it, it can happen. As a forest is made up of individual tress, so society is composed of individuals. If there is love in the heart of the individual, there is love in the home and if there is love in the home, there will be love in society. What I hope is clear is that the possibility, and therefore the responsibility, for achieving this lies with no-one else but ourselves.

5

GENERATING A FIERY HEART { ELIMINATING THE OBSTRUCTIONS

HOW MUCH DO I LOVE?

To develop a heart that truly loves and so to generate the elixir of life that can change our whole being, we have to eliminate those things in our personal and subconscious nature that either prevent or restrict it from unfolding. If we don't, our inner life – how we feel and react to life – will not change very much. We will stray no further than the limits of our comfort zones and will fail to realise our true nature. Life will not be lived to the full and our ability to give our full presence to others will be hampered. Even if we say to ourselves, "Yes, I do want to do this," resistance is bound to surface in us from time to time. Sometimes resistance will arise in the form of avoidance – finding other things to distract us – or as denial, such as when we think that something doesn't apply to us or does not exist.

In this chapter, we will look at some of the common basic causes that prevent or hinder the expression of love in all but the rarest of human beings. More importantly, we will look at methods which can help very much in breaking them down or dissolving them. It all requires work, of course. If an intellectual understanding were all that were needed, we would have an enlightened world already. Effort beyond reading the words is essential – but the rewards are immeasurable.

A GOOD FIRST STEP – A SIMPLE EXERCISE OF ANALYSIS

Draw a circle on a piece of paper. The circle need not be perfect but it should be reasonable in size. Then place a dot in the middle of it, like so:

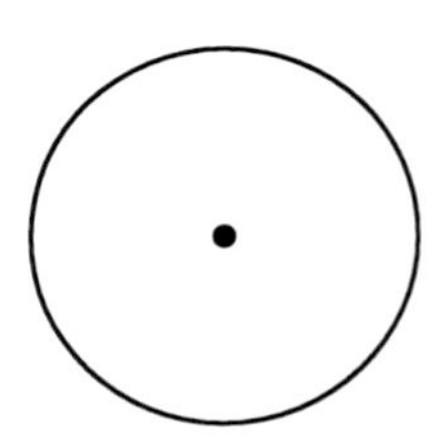

- In this exercise, the dot represents you and the circle represents the world you live in – your environment and everything in it that you can influence directly or indirectly.

- You can also mark within the circle – perhaps dots that are smaller or of a different colour – people, organisations and services that you come into contact with. Some will be closer to you than others.

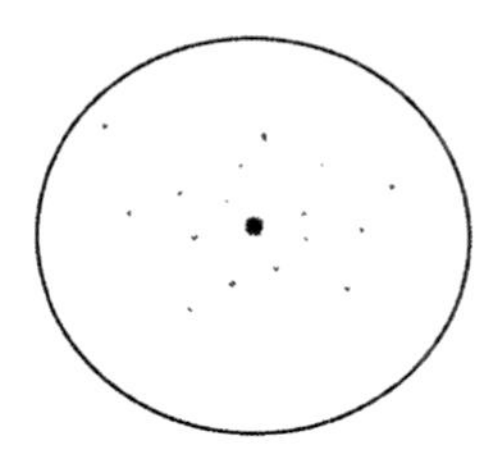

- Now draw or shade in the extent to which you think or feel that love normally extends from you into that environment. Bear in mind who and what comprise it but don't think *too* much about it at this stage. A spontaneous reaction is better and likely to be more intuitive.

- You will probably end up with an irregular shape but whatever shape it is doesn't matter. The important thing is that it means something to you and represents your view of how you love your world.

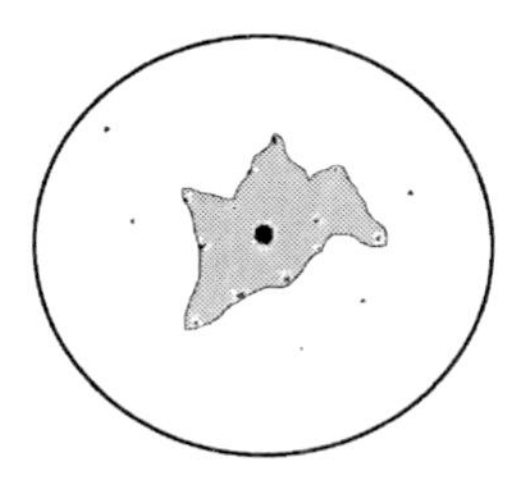

If you have done this with full honesty (and the honesty is for yourself, no-one else) there will be a considerable amount of the circle that is not included in your love and that is normal. But what does the excluded part signify?

In essence, it represents a gap or gaps in consciousness. Where love is present, there is a bridge in consciousness; love has a unifying effect. You cannot love someone unless your consciousness embraces them to some degree and that extension of consciousness is entirely positive. It is constructive rather than destructive in nature. If we have negative feelings towards someone, then our consciousness is faulty and has a damaging effect on our well-being. So we could say that if there is love, our consciousness is healthy and if there is hatred, jealousy or other negative thoughts and emotions there is an unhealthy state.

Perhaps that is obvious but most of us have a vast area where there is neither a positive nor a negative attitude. That area is rather grey and could probably best be described as neutral indifference. We may say that that is fine because surely no harm is coming from it, but do we really want to make do with fine? That indifference is where our consciousness is lacking in vitality; it is numb or asleep.

So our diagram shows us where we need to revitalise or awaken ourselves and this is nothing other than the process of enlightenment. Our aim, and it is a lifelong one, should be to fill that whole circle with love, with positivity and joy. Nothing less will do if we want to realise our true nature and so release the full potential of the elixir of life that resides within us.

Why is there such a gap or interruption in our consciousness that we exclude more than we include in our awareness? Surely awareness is simply that and, by definition, must include everything? If we had perfect, absolute clarity that may be so but in practice our awareness needs to expand. A child may be able to read but only certain books are likely to be within its grasp and in a sense we are like children, with a capacity for only so much. Beyond a certain limit, things are meaningless. So it is with our capacity for love. However, even though that may be limited, there is much we can do to expand it significantly in a relatively short time. If we are going to do that, it is important to understand why we have such enormous gaps.

Each of us has a fundamental error in our perception leading to quite extraordinary beliefs; these restrict us and cause no end of pain, misery and suffering. That error is that we see ourselves as separate individuals. Each of us has a strong sense of *I, me* and *mine*. We have our own distinct boundaries that we impose in the belief that they protect us, although the truth is that they cause no end of trouble. In the diagram of our simple exercise, the dot is the "I" and the shaded area is the extent to which we are prepared to extend our boundaries. Everything outside of the boundaries is very much "out there" – apparently not part of us. Even within the inner or shaded area, there is unlikely to be unity of consciousness but rather an acceptance of being connected or related to what is there.

This sense of separateness is said to be the *basic ignorance* which is usually described in a somewhat pictorial way by religious traditions as a fall from grace or, in Judaeo-Christian terms, as original sin. These, rather unhelpfully I think, imply some sort of blame for the condition we all find ourselves in. It is better, perhaps, using another pictorial expression, to recognise that we are in the dark and need to turn the light on. For those seeking a more analytical approach to how ignorance arises in consciousness, a look at the twelve stages of unenlightenment as propounded in the Dzogchen teachings of Buddhism can be most illuminating.[16]

For our purposes, the essence that is helpful to understand is that from the initial sense or belief that "I am me and distinct from all else", we favour those things that support "me" and disfavour those things we perceive as threatening to "me". You may say that you never consciously think like that but this is a very basic tendency in our psyche that governs our perceptions and reactions. From this tendency, the basic psychological patterns of attachment and aversion arise – I like this but dislike that and so on. At their most primeval state, they give rise to the survival instinct and following Maslow's famous theory of needs[17] become ever more complex and sophisticated as our needs are fulfilled.

Attachment on the one hand and aversion on the other

---

16 See "The twelvefold chain of interdependent causation of samsara" – *The Practice of Dzogchen* p.54 by Longchen Rabjam, translated by Tulku Thondup, edited by Harold Talbott, Snow Lion Publications 1989 & 1996; *The Meaning of Life,* The Dalai Lama, translated and edited by Jeffrey Hopkins, Wisdom Books 1989.

17 See Abraham Maslow, *A Theory of Human Motivation, Psychological Review* (1943), 370–396, expanded in *Motivation and Personality*, Harper & Row, 1954.

are a little bit like positive and negative poles in an electrical circuit and the reaction between the two governs how we react. We would find it difficult to survive as human beings without them, at least to some degree, because fear can keep us from danger, aversion to hunger ensures we eat and so on. As we shall look at in a moment, they undoubtedly create difficulties for us; but it is the third state, indifference, which can be the most problematic in our quest to expand the qualities of the heart. If you have completed the circle diagram exercise, much of the gap, if not most of it, is likely to be because of this condition rather than aversion or dislike. Most people in the world are what might be said to be off our radar screens and, quite fairly, you could say that it is impossible to be aware of all the people in the world. However, think of being in a busy place – walking in a town centre, for example – and ask yourself to what extent you would feel a close connection with the other people milling around or driving past. It isn't the fact that we don't have any negative feelings towards them that is significant; it is the fact that the vast majority of people don't have any feelings towards most of the rest of humanity whatsoever. That isn't a criticism but an observation of fact. The wonderful thing, though, is that we can do something about that so far as our own development is concerned and when we do we will find bubbles of joy rising up in our consciousness. The magic of the world will unveil itself to us and we will begin to realise our divine nature and that of every other living being.

The sun of our hearts is really the potential of our consciousness that seeks expression. Our consciousness *wants* to blossom; it wants to radiate and illumine our lives and our surroundings. That is our natural state. While there is anything in the way, blocking that natural inner light, there is probably some discomfort and certainly a feeling of lack at some level. Those who are truly fulfilled are very few in number. Unless we are totally overcome with inertia, until we realise our full potential there will always be a drive within us to seek something more. The something is not in the outside world and if we go looking for it there, we will become tired and perhaps a little disheartened. People who genuinely lead fulfilling lives are those who are following their own path; in other words, they are following their natural course of evolution and are doing what is right for them at their particular stage. For some that might be motherhood, for another being an artist or musician, for another following a profession and for some the fulfilment of simply engaging in hard work. No-one can say what is right for another person and we should never criticise the path in life someone is following. However, a growing number of people have discovered that a development of the heart consciousness is so very right. This means breaking down many of the blockages that impede it.

These blockages arise from the three prongs of basic ignorance that have been mentioned – attachment, aversion and indifference. Due to attachment, we try to draw things to us that we like, that make us feel good or that boost our self-esteem. So desires arise. This tendency isn't limited to things and also includes people and circumstances. We try to draw everything to us and, as the fulfilment of desires is pleasurable, once they are satisfied, further desires arise. Many desires are short-lived and cause little trouble – mere whims that drift into our lives and drift out again. Others are stronger and if they are not fulfilled there is often frustration or disappointment.

When attachment leads to desire there is an interesting effect in energy terms. Whereas when our heart is filled with loving kindness there is expansion and radiance, desire is like a prong going out with a hook or a sucker on the end, drawing in when it reaches its target. There is a great contraction of energy. If you can imagine a sea anemone suddenly pulling its tentacles in when a fish touches them and drawing everything into itself, it's a little like that. If we live like that habitually, a pattern of energy is formed and so it becomes more difficult to express love and kindness. The mind follows habitual patterns and, when these are entrenched, it is very difficult to break out of them. These patterns of continually drawing things to ourselves create obstructions to expressing love. It's not that we become incapable; it's that our mind and emotions need retraining so that they can take on a different shape or a different movement. Rather than sending out prongs or tentacles to find short-lived satisfaction from other people and things, the plucking needs to be from the treasure trove that lies within us and, finding the gems there, giving them out. This reversal of attitude, and therefore of energy, is what generates the elixir of life; it generates tremendous joy and happiness and, incidentally, is far more likely to bring a genuine lustre to the complexion than the potions cosmetic companies and others try to lure us into buying! The habitual tendency of the mind to want to gather things is one of the main obstacles to our natural expression and to our happiness. Recognising this is a major step in the process of creating a fiery heart.

Far more complex and difficult to identify are the myriad emotions and consequent thought processes that result from the basic tendency of aversion to anything perceived as threatening to "me" and all its attributes. Most of the negative emotions come in here, from pride and jealousy to anger and hatred. We may say that we don't suffer from them very often but they have many subtle variations and it is these that are so pernicious and difficult to root out. In Buddhism it is said that there are 84,000 negative or afflictive emotions;[18] fear is one of the greatest forms of aversion and its expressions are beyond counting.

Every type of aversion causes a shrinking in our energy. It is easy to understand fear and disgust, for example, as having this type of result. What is less obvious, is the effect in someone who appears very active and outgoing – too much so, perhaps – but who harbours negative emotions inside. A person who is bombastic, blustering or arrogant appears to give out a great deal of energy; but what is being given out is superficial, even if it is forceful, and marks an absence of the

---

18 I don't suppose for a minute that anyone has ever counted them and that figure is probably symbolic as much as anything. Nevertheless, the number must be very great.

glorious manifestation of the love and energy that comes from an expansive heart. An extrovert, the life and soul of the party and apparently very outgoing, can nevertheless have a great deal of tightness inside and that tightness can be vice-like. All of us have a certain degree of this and one measure of how closed or open we are is the extent to which we are naturally kind.

Just so we are clear, openness or tightness in this context is a mental–emotional state rather than a physical one. Nevertheless, there is a wide (if not universal) acceptance that our mental and emotional states impinge on the physical body. From everyday experience, we know that our sense of well-being changes with our moods and that mental tension creates physical tension. Our pulse rate, blood pressure and biochemical balance are all affected by how we are thinking and feeling. The important thing, though, is not whether we are occasionally tense or feel a little negative but how our thinking and moods are as a general trend.

SOME EXAMPLES OF BLOCKAGES

It is easy to identify the negative or afflictive psychological states when they are displayed or felt grossly. We usually know if we are feeling very angry and can often see when someone else is (although we cannot know exactly how they are feeling). If we act in a very haughty manner, we may be honest enough to realise later that pride had taken a grip; we will also know that it adversely affected our judgement, our thoughts and possibly our speech and behaviour, too. On the other hand, pride may blind us to many of the faults we have.

At this point I would like to digress slightly because the use of the word "fault" in this context causes some people problems. They say, or perhaps have read or heard somewhere, that we are all perfect as we are and that it is a little negative to say we have faults. They are entitled to that view, as is the person who runs an old motor vehicle that pollutes the environment with very dirty exhaust fumes and claims it is a perfect runner. I am using the word fault here to mean that, without attributing blame in any direction, there is something that can be improved upon. We all have psychological issues of one sort or another and there is no point at all in blaming anyone or anything for them. They are there and, whilst they are, they are preventing us from expressing our full nature. Eradicating these faults is a long process but it is possible to tackle them and many, if not most, will disappear as we develop a more positive approach to life.

We can speed this process up if we know that how we are thinking is not correct, so identifying negative or harmful thought patterns has great value. Let us take a look at two or three examples of gross and obvious ways of wrong thinking which have subtler twists and shades that are not nearly so easy to spot. It is often the subtle aspects, together with their emotional responses, that are the most difficult to uproot and so can be very problematical.

Greed and its cousin, *avarice,* cause immense difficulty and suffering in the world. They always have and, unless and until humanity changes, they always will. They are the antithesis to love and a person who is greedy or mean is far from happy. Globally, humanity is not a happy race. Economic imbalance is extreme. However, this wouldn't be the case if love predominated, and the only way we can change the world is by changing ourselves. If we want to do something about the effects of greed and avarice in the human family, we have to eliminate all traces of them within ourselves as individuals, rather than taking the easy way out of pointing the finger of blame at other people or even other nations. We may say, "Well, that's fine – I'll eat a little less chocolate or not buy so many clothes." The subtler aspects of these mental pollutants, though, require a little closer self-examination and more than a modicum of honesty. Suppose, for example, that a bill for goods or services we have purchased is wrong. Probably we will be quick enough to point out the error if we have been over-charged; but are we just as quick to say if we have been *under*-charged? Is there any thought that we might have done rather well out of the transaction or, indeed, the slightest hesitation in putting it right? Some people would say that it's not up to them and that it was the vendor's fault. If we have a tendency to think like that, we need to do a little work on our loving kindness.

Pride is often associated with arrogance or a big ego but it, too, has subtle tones that take some digging out. We may not be pompous but perhaps we enjoy receiving praise for a job well done or even expect some recognition for what we have achieved. It is important to praise others but to seek it for oneself means that there is a little work to be done. Do we like to be well-regarded by other people? If we do, we may be suffering from a hint of pride. Do we like to be proved right and would we ever conceal a mistake? It's there again. Humility is sometimes thought of as a weakness but the truly humble person has no pride sticking to them at all.

Anger is easy to spot when it is strong or gross and it may be that we rarely become angry. To think there is nothing to remedy, though, may be to look upon things a little too shallowly. Are we so pure that resentment could never arise, resentment over some injustice, for example? In terms of mental equanimity, resentment, taking offence, feeling cross, indignant or hurt and so on are all subtle shades of anger and each of them detracts from our natural clarity.

We could progress through many of the major emotions and mental states at different levels. One approach in tantric Buddhism is to meditate on each of the main states at varying degrees of expression – great, middle and small.[19] Once they are identified, it becomes easier to rid oneself of them. Thorough and helpful though that approach may be, you can imagine that if we followed that method, it would take a very long time indeed. We would probably become discouraged quite early on and end up abandoning the exercise. In any event, most of us do not have sufficient leisure time to spend long periods in deep reflection. The purpose of highlighting this topic is simply to understand, in a slightly different way, why we are such complex psychological machines and that, if we are to enjoy life to the full and realise our spiritual potential, there is a considerable amount of garbage that needs to be transformed. The transformation process is a long one but is made a little easier

---

19 Each of these is subdivided into great, middle and small, so there are nine levels from the grossest to the most subtle.

if we can understand that all these afflictive emotions and mental states have their root in the three fundamental bases of attachment, aversion and ignorance or indifference. In turn, these three arise from the ego with its sense of "I, me and mine". The more quickly we can eradicate the "I", the greater the transformation, and love is a key factor, if not *the* factor, in this process.

I LIKE YOU, I DON'T LIKE YOU, I'M NOT BOTHERED

Many Eastern teachers are amazed at how much extra preliminary work needs to be undertaken with western students before any real progress can be made with meditation. As a society, we are really "into ourselves" and tend to regard ourselves, our foibles and neuroses as being the centre of the universe. There is a growing trend, too, to showcase various psychoses in so-called reality television programmes and in other types of media – newspapers, books, magazines and the internet. The more extreme the case in hand, the better the entertainment value, it seems, and the sufferer often basks in the glory of a few minutes of fame whilst the observer can safely feel how wonderful it is to be "normal". No wonder society has its problems.

Whilst this isn't a book aimed at overcoming specific psychological states, in our quest to open the heart to love, it can be very helpful to understand how some of these states arise and how they prevent us from expressing love as fully as our inner, spiritual nature is capable of doing. It is because of them that the human personality is often fickle and that from liking someone it is possible to change into not wanting anything to do with them. Indeed, in many spiritual traditions it is said that it is easy for a friend to become one's enemy in a very short time.

So it is that we are drawn towards people when there is something attractive about them or that makes us feel comfortable with them – we looked at this in the context of relationships in chapter 2 – and are repelled by others. It becomes awfully complicated because there are so many permutations that come in. For example, A might like B because B appears to possess factors u, v, w, x, y & z but dislikes C because C appears to possess factors p, q, r, s & t. Both B & C would probably be totally unaware of the qualities that A was seeing in them. In psychoanalysis, the underlying causes for A's perception of p, q, r, s & t in C might be investigated, revealing that each of those factors might have roots in other factors and so on. Psychoanalysis can be very helpful in specific cases but it is easy to see that to unearth every little cause that makes us unhappy and prevents the expression of love would be a very laborious process. For our spiritual expansion we need something much easier. If we are to fill our circle (the exercise in the first section of this chapter) we need to work a little faster. To focus on every single cause for all our negative and indifferent feelings would be like filling a bucket with grains of sand using only a pair of tweezers. It is also important to understand and fully take on board our areas of indifference to the billions of other members of the human race towards whom we may have little or no feeling unless some tragedy befalls them. This is all those people for whom we have no feelings of dislike but no feelings of warmth either. Spiritually, and in terms of awareness, we are numb or asleep but it *is* possible to wake this part of us up relatively quickly.

THE FIERY HEART HAS EQUAL LOVE FOR ALL

The fiery heart that is within each of us waiting to be expressed does not distinguish between one person and another. Like the sun, it simply shines. It takes time to develop and there are essentially two things that must be done. One is to increase its brightness or strength and the other is to remove all obstacles within us that cast shadows and so prevent the sunlight – the love of the fiery heart – from reaching everywhere.

These days, everyone expects instant results but to expect instant enlightenment inevitably leads to disappointment. Many people go to introductory sessions on meditation, for example, but comparatively few possess the patience to continue and so they go on to try something else, and then something else again. Like most things in life worth the effort, *true* spiritual development takes application. You cannot become an Olympic swimmer by enjoying a paddle at the seaside or even by swimming just a few widths or lengths of the municipal baths. However, unlike many things in life that require persistent training, development of the heart need not, and indeed should not, interfere with normal everyday activities.

The challenge ahead, then, is to dissolve the countless obstacles in our mental–emotional make-up in order that the fiery heart within us can become truly awake. Two thoughts of encouragement: (1) if we place one foot after another and proceed one step at a time, enjoying the journey, we will arrive at our destination; and (2) as the warmth in the heart grows, obstacles begin to melt.

DEVELOPING A CORRECT VIEW

There is a truism that says the world is as we are. The only world we can ever know is the one we experience through our senses, our perceptions, beliefs, judgements and so on. How the world is to anyone depends on their view and, due to the vacillations of the mind and the emotions, that view inevitably changes, often many times a day.

If we are driving a car, the view of the road will depend on a number of factors. The windscreen needs to be kept clear, our eyesight good and our focus and attention must be on where we are going. Similarly, in life our view of what is in front of us must also be clear. In our overall theme of developing the heart, there are two things in particular that we should pay attention to as far as our view is concerned. One is how we see ourselves and the other is how we see other people. Those two views are like two sides of a coin – there cannot be one without the other and each necessarily depends on the other – and both are affected very deeply by the state of "basic ignorance" we spoke of earlier.

To develop love – or more accurately to allow love to flourish – we have to begin to alter the state whereby we view ourselves as separate entities, and as totally separate from the rest of the universe. That also means that we have to alter our view of other people as being separate from each other and, indeed, separate from us. To change the way we see things is an enormous step but it is the single most important and significant thing we can ever do. Because it is so enormous, we have to undertake it carefully and remain focused. There will be countless times when we feel we have fallen backwards. We mustn't give up when that happens because, if we do so, we will simply "revert to type".

To start to change our perceptions of ourselves and others, a little gentle analysis can be extraordinarily helpful. If we are not yet ready to accept that none of us is really separate from everything else, let us try to see what it is about us that is solid or permanent. If we think logically about the body, we know that it is neither solid nor permanent. Everything about it is in a state of change. Nothing is more than a few months old yet we are so often fooled into thinking that the image in the bathroom mirror is "me". It isn't; it never was and never can be. Nor, if there is any inclination to think it, can "me" be the brain, which is simply part of the physical body.

Some people would say, "I can recognise that I am not my body so I must be my mind." The difficulty with that is that what is regarded as the mind cannot be pinpointed either. What we generally term *mind* is the sum total of our thoughts, beliefs, perceptions and so on – all of which are subject to change. If we take time to reflect on this, we will find that the mind is neither solid nor, more importantly, permanent. But we will also find that if the mind is stilled, awareness remains.

We can also reflect in a slightly different way. Not only is the body not permanent, it is made entirely of elements from within the universe. There is very keen interest these days in genealogy, the study of one's ancestral lineage. Perhaps it is a yearning to discover one's true source that motivates people to do this. What it shows is that our bodies are just one component in a long chain of events and, if one link were missing, our bodies could not exist now. But they are dependent on more than ancestry. Our bodies would not be here if it were not for food, clothing, shelter, the sun, the clouds, the earth and so on. Everything about us depends on something else. Our beliefs, thoughts and perceptions, all that we could call our mental and emotional make-up, also have preceding causes without which we would not be as we are.

It is extraordinarily productive to think about this and to take some time out now and again to enjoy – yes, enjoy – reflecting on our interdependent and impermanent nature.

An extraordinarily liberating meditation

Sit in a comfortable position in a place where you will not be disturbed; it is usually better to close the eyes so as not to be distracted by the surroundings. Spend a few minutes reflecting on each of the following thoughts:

- *I am not my body; my body is not me. It is forever changing, just like the water of a river.*
- *I am not my thoughts; my thoughts are not me. Like clouds in the sky, they appear, change and move on.*
- *I am not my feelings or emotions; feelings and emotions are not me. Like the waves of the ocean, they arise and disappear.*
- *I am not my perceptions. How I interpret and experience what I see, hear, feel, smell and taste depends on many causes, none of which are permanent.*
- *I am not my beliefs, prejudices and preconceptions and they are not me. They arise from nothingness and dissolve back into nothingness. They are without substance.*
- *Beyond all this is a state of pure awareness, boundless and pristine, from which arises fathomless love, wisdom and compassion. This is my real nature.*

If there is insufficient time to go through all the stages of the meditation, you can focus on just one or two. Please don't expect an instantaneous change from just one reflection. This is a gentle process that takes time. It is a little bit like cultivating a garden that has grown wild. Patient tending will produce results but, if after a while we become bored and give up, the weeds will simply take over again.

A POWERFUL TECHNIQUE TO CHANGE OUR PERSPECTIVE

The second strand that is very useful involves employing the imagination. It is a technique that is used in some Buddhist practices but doesn't require us to be a Buddhist in order to do it. Whatever religion or culture we have been brought up in, the technique is extraordinarily powerful and transformative. Its purpose is to break down or pierce through the mental boundaries we have created in seeing others as separate from us. Use of the imagination is a legitimate tool for transforming the mind and in this method we use the mind to introduce some extra feeling in the heart; in fact, we are going to apply a match and ignite it! To do this, you need to be able to see someone or bring someone to mind.

- *Imagine that the person in your view or in your thoughts was, at some time in the far distant past, very close to you and cared for you very deeply. That relationship has been forgotten – lost in the mists of time – but imagine that you remember it now. (Of course, we must never disclose that we are doing this because it would probably disturb the other person – this is simply a mental technique.)*

If you apply this technique diligently, you will notice feelings being stirred within you and that a link of sorts will build up between you. Actually, all that is happening is that you are enlivening what is already there. The boundaries we have created in the mind that make us feel everything is separate from us are false – they have no substance. In terms of our spiritual development, however, they feel real and solid, like an invisible shield.

Some people worry about doing something like this. "What if I interfere with the other person's energy?" or "If it is an unpleasant person, do I open myself to their energy?" are questions that can come up. The answer is "no" on both counts and to any similar questions. What we are doing is expanding our consciousness a little and so opening up the possibility of love where it was absent or increasing it if it was there.

Because the effects of this exercise are quite strong, some people find it too difficult to maintain all the time. If they do continue with it, a point comes when it doesn't seem to work anymore. This may be because they have become a little blasé about it – the novelty has worn off – but often it is due to some inner resistance building. Either way, this technique seems to be more effective if it is done periodically for short periods which can be increased very gradually. It is, though, worth the small effort involved because it will bring very real, and very enjoyable, results.

A DIVINE WHOLENESS

A growing realisation comes that all boundaries occur in the mind and that consciousness is whole. Gradually, a feeling that everything is divine may arise. In this secular age, use of terms such as "the divine" can cause a little resistance. This is a great shame because when that happens, it is like sitting in a room with one's back to the window, oblivious to a marvellous vista and even denying it is there.

Let us just say for now that everything is a *magnificent wholeness*. Wholeness, by definition, is indivisible but our minds have split up every appearance of wholeness and created a false image of multiplicity. Everything has to be named or labelled, given an identity, because our minds struggle with the concept (or rather "conceptlessness") of wholeness. Religions try to overcome this but for many people they fail because of the innate tendency to label everything as "this" or "that", "God" and "not God" and so they don't find wholeness – just a different form of multiplicity.

My invitation to you is, if you have any resistance to the concept of the divine or to divinity (and most of us have at some level) to remember that the divine is simply a term for *magnificent wholeness*. There is no need to label everything, to classify and to name. Such things are modes of communication between minds. Regard everything, absolutely everything, as magnificent wholeness. The mind will relax and inner tensions will ease because recognition – *knowing again* – of a deeper truth begins to arise. When that happens, the glow of the fiery heart brightens.

6

THE IMPORTANCE OF LIVING MINDFULLY

MINDFULNESS – ESTABLISHING A PRESENCE

Love requires our presence. A mother, for example, cannot love her child without awareness of the child and the more fully present and aware she is, the greater her capacity for love is in that moment. Love without awareness is impossible; full love without full awareness is likewise impossible. We take it for granted that we love those close to us but how often are we *fully* present with them?

Living mindfully means continually having our awareness fully in the present moment. So, if someone is speaking to us, our awareness should be fully on them and what they are saying. In practice, most people find that the mind wanders even when they are concentrating on what is being said – something that the speaker says starts a new train of thought in the listener or the listener wants to say something and so concentration lapses. At that point, of course, there is no listener – just the appearance of one. The speaker, on the other hand, may also be lacking presence. If we are talking to someone, we should be totally aware of the other person and of their listening. If we are aware of them, we will also be aware when their attention has wandered and will do something to bring them back to us.

Mindful living is not easy because it means overcoming the habitual tendency that we all have to be partly absent from whatever we are doing. But if we want to be really happy, we have to love and, in order to love, we have to be fully present. Actually, although it is not easy to be mindful, it is the simplest thing in the world because, instead of doing more, we have to do less. Most things in life require us to act. Therefore, in order to achieve anything, it seems we have to do more. Then we either become hooked in the spiral of doing more and more, or else we become disheartened or feel guilty because we haven't achieved what we think we should have. Fortunately, there is a middle way. Mindful living is not so much about *doing* things as about *being*. We simply have to be in order to *be* a full human being. Being busy can be very good, of course, and activities have to take place otherwise the world as we know it would not exist. Through our various occupations, we learn skills and serve our fellow human beings. This is all good. But most people are so active in their minds that they find it very difficult to be still; even when the opportunity comes to sit and do nothing for a short time, the majority of folk will look for something to do.

Our modern world does not particularly support mindfulness, either. Despite technology that enables almost anything that we could wish for to be achieved or obtained, our modern lifestyle detracts from an environment that encourages mindfulness. We are bombarded at every turn by stimuli – advertising, radio, television, mobile telephones, e-mails, the internet and so on. All these things have their virtues but, like anything in life, excess is not good. The modern mind generally works too fast because it races from one thing to another without paying a great deal of attention to almost anything. One major effect of this is that we are not generally very good at loving.

All is not lost, however. No matter how busy we are or think we are, it is possible to become more mindful. It doesn't matter whether a person has an IQ of 70 or 150; it is possible for everyone to enjoy greater awareness – and so greater fulfilment – in life. In fact, sometimes people with very active intellects find it more difficult at first because their minds are always arguing, forever differentiating between this and that, and making judgements. But, like monetary wealth, more of something does not always bring greater happiness and an overactive intellect is a case in point. Nevertheless, once the purity of natural awareness is experienced, the joy – and relief – is equally great for everyone.

LOVE IS MORE THAN PEOPLE

At the end of the last chapter, we touched on the idea of there being a magnificent wholeness and, if we can warm to the idea that all people and everything in the environment are different aspects of that magnificent wholeness, we might also be receptive to the thought that being mindful in all our activity can release our full potential. This means that love, which inevitably arises as a result of mindful presence, becomes a factor – and eventually becomes *the* factor – in absolutely everything we turn our minds to. That may be a huge distance from wherever we are now, but we can cover it gradually, just a little step at a time. If that still seems impossible, think back to the little exercise we completed at the beginning of chapter 5. All that is being suggested here is to enlarge the smaller area represented in the middle of that diagram so that, little by little, it encompasses the whole. In other words, gradually and patiently, we extend our love a little further, beyond its current limits. And in the same way that it isn't necessary to do anything other than provide a seed with the correct growing conditions to produce a plant, mindfulness provides the correct, and totally natural, conditions of life which will gradually produce the full flower of love in our hearts.

MINDFULNESS IN DAILY ACTIVITY

We are now going to look at a number of ideas as to how mindfulness and love can be brought into daily activity. If you already do these things, or some of them, you may find that reading about them will strengthen what you do now. For those for whom this is an entirely new approach, please don't think that you have to do all of them. It is often better to begin with one or two and increase a little at a time than to try to do everything at once.

- *Waking*

When we awaken in the morning, it is so easy to let the mind wander and, if that happens, our energy becomes very untidy. Remember that the energy in the body responds to our mental state; if our mind is alert and focused, then, generally speaking, the body will respond accordingly whereas if the mind is fuzzy or all over the place, we know from experience that our energy level will not be good. An athlete only achieves top performance as a result of a focused mind and an archer will only hit the target if his mind is still and his body steady. Although most of us will not necessarily want to start the day bouncing with the energy of an athlete, to get out of bed in the mornings in a clear and happy frame of mind provides a good foundation for the rest of the day.

Instead of turning over and pulling the covers up, thinking, "I'll just have another couple of minutes," we can begin to gather our energy together. Unless there is some physical reason not to, it is better to lie on the back at this point and bring the awareness onto the whole body. Be aware of the movement of your breathing and smile to your body, filling it with goodness. Start at the heart and radiate warmth, kindness and love throughout the torso, the arms and hands, the legs and feet, then finally the head. After a few moments, fill the space immediately around you with the same goodness and extend it to the entire room. Appreciate the moment you are in; it is a miracle. Greet the day with a smile. Remember everything is an expression of magnificent wholeness and you are part of it. If you like to pray before you rise, this is a good time to do it; some people like to do small exercises to loosen their joints a little. Whatever you do, do it with full awareness but do not linger too long, otherwise the mind will start to wander and that is to be avoided. So, as soon as you are ready, gently rise.

- *Rising*

Getting out of bed should be a wonderful moment. If we have woken mindfully, it will be – unless, of course, the mind becomes distracted. It is very easy for that to happen and if we simply follow a normal routine "on autopilot", just rolling out from under the covers without thinking, the magic of the present moment will be lost. Having filled our space with goodness, it can work well to sit on the edge of the bed for a few moments. Be conscious of the body and feel as though light is radiating from you, filling not only the room you are in but the whole building as well. Feel as though that light is filling the whole day ahead of you and be glad you are where you are. This is a wonderful moment to fill your entire day with blessedness. Be grateful for all that you have and then stand slowly, with full awareness, and maintain a smile. Such a beginning to the day can bring amazing results and, if we are interrupted, it is important not to mind but to simply bless the interruption from the heart. It may take a little effort to bring this into our routine, but once it becomes established it is very easy to do and very worthwhile. From time to time, vary your focus so that your awareness remains fresh and doesn't fall into old habits. Remember that there are no hard and fast rules to any of these suggestions – they need to be enjoyable, so alter them as you wish.

- *Ablutions*

The morning trip to the bathroom may not be an event we think about very much. After all, we've been doing it since we were tiny and it doesn't take a great deal of planning to take a shower or a bath, have a wash, clean our teeth or use the lavatory. Nevertheless, if we want to maintain mindfulness in life and to love fully, there is a great deal to be gained by increasing our awareness in this part of the morning's routine – or, indeed, at any other time that we enjoy the fruits of modern plumbing and water supply. In fact, as appreciation is part of mindfulness, it is not a bad idea to remember that most people in the world do not have plumbed water supply or sanitation and that what we enjoy and take for granted is a privilege.

Rather than ploughing straight into normal routine, try pausing for a few seconds on entering the bathroom; take one or two breaths and appreciate your surroundings, no matter whether they be plush or meagre. Take a moment, as on rising, to fill the room with light and goodness; then proceed slowly and with full awareness of your every move. This is crucial to maintaining awareness: have your full awareness on and in every movement of your legs and feet, arms and hands.

When using the lavatory, rather than letting the mind

wander over this and that, be aware that you are returning earth and water elements to the Earth. They will be transformed and reused; be grateful for the use you have had of them and return them happily. This may sound odd if you haven't thought on these lines before. The physical process is, after all, the same whether we think this way or not. What we are doing, though, is using every moment we can to transform the mind so that it is vital and aware, appreciative, kind and compassionate.

Water is a vital and precious commodity and deserves to be treated with reverence, so try to do so as you wash yourself or bathe. Treat everything you use in the bathroom with care and appreciation and as you clean the body, regard it as a valuable vehicle that needs to be looked after carefully. If your health is not good, imagine that you are healing the body as you wash it and dry it; if you are healthy, appreciate your fortune and respect the body as you perform your ablutions.

When you are done, don't simply rush out of the door. Turn and pause with a moment of gratitude and leave the room slowly and mindfully.

- *Meditation*

Increasing numbers of people are finding that beginning the day with a short period of meditation[20] brings enormous benefits which significantly improve the quality of life. Although most meditations can be done anywhere, to have

---

20 See Appendix for two meditations.

a quiet spot in the home is very pleasant and can help us settle more easily. Rather than a sitting meditation, some prefer to practise some gentle movement such as t'ai chi or chi kung. Whatever our preference, some peaceful minutes will strengthen our awareness and soothe the nervous system, so getting the day off to a stress-free start. The good sense of that should be obvious but in our quest for developing the beautiful quality of love, which in reality is all about discovering our true nature, it is important to start the day as we mean to go on – peacefully. If you do not already enjoy the benefit of some quiet minutes, please think about introducing it into your morning routine; you will reap more from that time than, for example, from having the radio or television on. Having cleansed the body, we can spend some time bathing the mind.

It is very helpful to go into this period with appropriate mindfulness. Rather than just sitting down and beginning our meditation, on entering the room or part of the home where we are going to sit, it is good to pause and fill the room with goodness. Treat it as a sacred space. Form the intention that the next few minutes will be dedicated to quietness and to meditation. Breathe gently and sit down with deliberate slowness; take a few moments to be aware of your position in the room and your posture and then gently begin the meditation. If you have not learnt a meditation, you can sit quietly with eyes closed and with awareness lightly resting on the rhythm of the breath.[21]

---

21 See Appendix for a more detailed description.

The same principle applies if the preference is for some light exercise – be aware of your space and dedicate it to your practice. Always allow a few moments of quietness, with awareness on the body and the breathing before beginning – and then thoroughly enjoy what you do.

On finishing, take a moment or two to appreciate the space you are in and be grateful for the opportunity you have had. Then move easily and without haste onto whatever you need to do next.

- *Clothes*

The principle of mindfulness should apply to everything we do and that includes our attitude to our clothes and the way we put them on. Although the main purpose of clothing may be said to protect the body, it also affects how we present ourselves to the rest of the world. If we feel badly about what we wear or cannot be bothered about how we look, it can adversely affect our self-esteem and that seriously weakens our capacity to love. It is difficult to love if we are not happy and we cannot be happy if our self-esteem is low.

Whether we can afford many clothes or very few, we should feel good about what we do have. Appreciation uplifts our spirits no end and to appreciate something properly requires our full awareness. So whether we choose something to wear from a selection or pick up the only item of clothing that we have, we will gain so much if we pause for a moment and allow our awareness to rest on the garment. However modest or grand our clothing is, it only appears in our wardrobe as a result of a long and complicated chain of events – causative conditions. Many, many people have been involved in the design, creation and supply of every single item. The sun, the rain and the earth are all contributory factors and, whatever factor we think of, each has its own endless chain. It is not an exaggeration to say that the shirt or piece of underwear in our hands is a product and a reflection of the universe, of nature and of humanity. As such, it surely deserves our full attention and appreciation. Even if what we are about to put on is very old, we should have a feeling of gratitude for it. Then we can dress mindfully, with care and with a happy heart. As a result, we will naturally pay attention to how we appear; we will have respect for the clothes we wear and respect for ourselves. We will have respect for the world.

- *Preparing and eating meals*

Enjoying a meal is a very special time and both preparation of the meal and how we eat it have an effect not only on the physical body but on our state of consciousness, too. Sadly, most meals are prepared without full awareness, which means they are prepared without love, and most are also eaten mindlessly. If we prepare food in a hurry or, worse, in a bad or stressed mood, the most important ingredient is missing. In its approach to eating, today's society seems to have lost much of its reverence or respect towards food. In many homes, meals are no longer taken at a table; in many it is rare to eat without the television or radio on. In town centres it is not uncommon to see office workers walking round the shops or streets whilst eating pasties or sandwiches they have bought for lunch. Some people like to read and eat at the same time and others prefer to talk on their telephones whilst absent-mindedly popping food into their multitasking mouths; there are those who can even manage to smoke a cigarette as well. The distraction we choose is a matter of personal taste, but sadly the food no longer appears to be a matter of taste at all.

We cannot change the habits of others but we can change our own. If we approach food with mindfulness, we begin to do something constructive about improving our state of consciousness. Preparation of meals should be seen as a privilege, a special time, and if we begin with the intention of cooking or preparing a meal with love, there is a very good chance that we will do it mindfully. We should have love and appreciation for the ingredients; we will then handle them with care. Those who practise t'ai chi or one of the healing arts know that the awareness tends to lead and enliven the vital energy of the body. When we hold something with full awareness, more chi or vital energy is in our hands and some of it is transferred. The quality of what we are holding is enhanced. Perhaps it may only be in a small way but any enhancement to the vitality of food must be a good thing. It is good also to use our implements and cooking vessels with a similar attitude. You may have had the experience of picking up something that belonged to someone else and, without there being any apparent logical explanation, not liking the feel of it. The opposite can also be the case. So it should make good sense to want to imbue our entire personal environment with a positive quality.

The other good reason is the effect on our consciousness and well-being. If you remember, there are three primary attitudes that we have towards people and things – positivity, negativity and indifference. To fill our whole world, and therefore our lives, with love we obviously have to overcome the last two – and indifference is in most people the greater of these. It may seem a minor matter, but unless we have at the least a respect for the things we use in life, there is an area of indifference that will hold us back and that will restrict the flow of the elixir of the heart that we wish to generate.

Whether we are preparing food or drink for others or for ourselves, we transform it into a gift when we do it with our full awareness, with love and with happiness in the heart. That may be difficult on occasions because we are feeling down or upset and an idealist might say that someone else should cook that day. Such a counsel of perfection is likely to be impracticable in many homes but what we can do when upset is to slow ourselves down and bring the awareness onto our breathing. Let the breath and the mind settle; be aware of your feelings but don't make anything of them – they are just there and will eventually go. Remind yourself that food is a gift from nature and that to handle it with love and gratitude will turn it into a healing medicine. Love is the greatest healer and why shouldn't you be an alchemist of the greatest sort, transforming the food you handle into golden nourishment?

To love, we have to accept that things are as they are and that includes ourselves. We need to accept that if we feel out of sorts, that's the way things are for the moment;

if we feel unable to love, that too is the way we feel for the moment. These feelings won't last because nothing is permanent in nature, so love yourself just the way you are; smile to yourself then smile to the items of food you are going to put together or cook. Smiling to food, or indeed anything, with love is the simplest form of blessing. Blessing is not the preserve of religions – a smile from the heart is enough and we can add a few kindly or appreciative thoughts if we wish. Once you have begun making the meal, smile from time to time and guard your awareness. If you catch your mind wandering onto other things, pause for a moment, smile and bring your attention back to what you are doing.

As for eating, the kindest thing we can do for ourselves is to sit down at a table or in a place that is reserved for eating and nothing else. Some households don't have a table at which family or friends eat and instead sit on a sofa or in an armchair, which is a shame. It is not good for the digestion if we are hunched over our food or are in a lounging position; sitting up reasonably straight is better for the stomach and the digestive processes, as well as the posture; it also encourages clearer awareness, which is a vital component of mindfulness.

It is good to have a moment or two of silence before beginning the meal because it settles the mind and the body and helps to bring us into the present. In that silence, a brief reflection of appreciation and gratitude will focus the mind and "warm the heart". The saying of grace may be a dying tradition these days but, if done, it is important that it is said with real meaning and not as a habitual repetition or as lip service; like any prayer, it will be felt more if expressed in a quiet atmosphere.

The meal should then simply be enjoyed. To do that, we should notice the colours and textures as well as the flavours and aroma. Each mouthful will yield its maximum enjoyment and nourishment only if chewed slowly and with full awareness, which is unlikely if we are poised ready to pop the next mouthful in while still chewing. Enjoying our food in this way will slow the meal down but it will help the digestion no end; we may also find we are satisfied with slightly less food. Of even greater significance, eating mindfully creates a happier state of mind because to be happy requires true appreciation of the moment we are in and it is easier to love when we are happy. No matter whether the food is grand or humble, we should try to generate a feeling of gratitude, which will help to generate a state of "ego-lessness" in us.

It should go without saying but it doesn't harm to mention it – television, radio, reading and other distractions are not compatible with mindful eating and divide the awareness. In Buddhist philosophy it is said that whatever we are doing, we should know that we are doing it. In this context "know" means to have full awareness. When we are eating, we should know we are eating; when we are watching television, we should know we are watching television and so on.

In finishing the meal, it enhances the experience and our mindfulness if we can sit for a minute or two before getting up from our seat. If we can sit a little longer, that is even better. After breakfast we may be short of time because we have to leave for work, college or school but it will pay dividends if we can at least pause for a few moments to appreciate the fact that we have been able to eat and feel grateful for it. Gradually, we should learn to adjust our routine a little so that breakfast, and indeed any meal, is never a rushed affair. In fact, as we become accustomed to living mindfully, we begin to realise that rushing anything means we have temporarily lost our presence.

- *Going places*

If we are able to walk, we can walk mindfully; if we can drive, mindfulness should come into that, too. But like many of our activities, we probably tend to move from one place to another, particularly around the home or place of work, with our minds elsewhere. Although it might seem a little unreasonable to suggest that we should have full awareness on our walking to the bathroom when we have an urgent need to go there, one of the points about living mindfully is that in general the sense of needing to do things urgently should gradually diminish. The mind should be calm even when immediate or prompt action is required. However, let's think for a minute or two about less urgent errands. Unless we are physically restricted, we probably move around a fair bit. In the home, we move not only from one room to another but from one part of a room to another. Perhaps we need something that's on a table or shelf several feet away; in all probability, our eyes will be on the object we want and our mental focus will simply be on retrieving it. That's normal because that's the way we habitually act; almost everybody would act in that way. There may be a better way, though – one that encourages mindfulness which itself cultivates a better and more complete state of consciousness. Remember that for fulfilment in life and for development of the heart qualities in particular, the ability to do things with our whole being is essential. If we simply go into retrieval mode, there is an aspect missing – we have lost awareness of ourselves because our focus is entirely on the object and taking hold of it. To move mindfully requires awareness of self, awareness of space and awareness of movement in space, as well as our contact with objects in it. Instead of simply rushing across the room to get what we want with a comparatively narrow focus, we can allow our consciousness to expand to fill the entire process. After all, expansion of the heart involves expansion of consciousness and there is no reason why our consciousness should not develop so that it fills every moment of our day.

How can we move from one side of the room to the other to fetch what we need? Let's assume we are seated and that we have determined that we need something – a book, for example. Be aware of the body and its posture. This only has to be brief but it helps. It also helps if we can be aware of the breath – not to concentrate on it, just to lightly place the awareness on it. Then we decide that we are going to move across the room in a mindful fashion to fetch the book. That simple thought – that we are going to do it mindfully – is very strengthening to this practice. Rising up from our seat can be done fairly slowly and then with deliberateness we can feel each step and the body's posture and movements as we walk across the room. As this should be very enjoyable rather than an indifferent experience, a light smile is helpful. Before picking the book up, it is good to pause for a second; then we can take it and feel it in the hands before walking back in the same way. On sitting down, we should have full consciousness of our movement and then resume a good posture. Is that a great deal to do? In terms of changing the focus of the mind, it is actually easier because there comes with it a relaxing of mental tension but it does take a little persistence to introduce this as a new method; our normal ways of doing things have taken a lifetime of habit to cultivate, after all! In terms of time, it will take only a few seconds longer. Yes – seconds, not minutes. Those extra few seconds will make an extraordinary difference to the quality of our lives and gradually we will find that we have more time than less. Mindfulness gives some enormous paybacks.

In walking to places, the principle is the same. Enjoy every step, every breath, every sight, smell and sound. Try not to hurry because when we hurry the mind is a little agitated or tense. The important thing is that we enjoy the present moment and that we are fully present in it. If our mind is on our destination or is mulling over other things as we walk, we lose the experience of our walking. Then we are absent and are missing out on the precious moments of our precious life. On the other hand, if we are truly alive, truly aware, we can fill ourselves and our environment with love. Love is the essential ingredient that brings real happiness and fills life with a wonderful sense of ease.

Walking is one thing but once behind the wheel of a vehicle it can be difficult to maintain mindfulness because for many people a different persona often takes over. Instead of enjoying the moment, there is a determined focus to reach the destination; obstructions can cause impatience and any possibility of a complete view of life – that everything, including ourselves, is magnificent wholeness – disappears into an unknown void as we see everything in our sight as separate from us. What hope can there be, therefore, for a state of mindfulness when driving? Actually, the situation is not hopeless at all because driving or riding a vehicle provides all manner of opportunity and, once the experience of doing it with full consciousness and mental ease is tasted, there will be a natural desire to make it the norm. Then the tendency to jump into the car or onto the motorbike and dash here and there will begin to wane. It will become an enjoyable experience instead of a chore, an opportunity to have a relaxed state of alertness in activity instead of a personal challenge.

The old adage of starting as you mean to go on is particularly apposite in the context of driving. As in all things, being grateful for what we have helps and, whether the vehicle we use is shiny and new or is a dilapidated one that has seen far better days, before getting into it we can pause, smile and take a breath. Having sat down, instead of starting the engine immediately it will help to maintain calmness and clarity of mind if we pause for a breath or two; we should remember the purpose of the journey we are about to undertake but also remember that if we drive in haste we will have forgotten the purpose of life – to live and love fully in the now. We can then make any preliminary checks and start the engine, again pausing to "breathe a smile" into the car before setting off. This should ensure that we commence the journey in something of a good mood and, with this air of positivity, we can proceed calmly and with an awareness that is truly alive. During the journey, imagining that we know the drivers of all the other vehicles we see on the road will help us maintain equanimity. Many people drive aggressively but there is no need to do so; it is just as easy – and so much better for everybody and the planet – if we drive with an air of friendliness and kindliness. More importantly, we will be guarding our consciousness and nurturing the heart. If someone in front of us is going too slowly, it is easy to feel a little irritated or frustrated if we are stuck behind them and cannot pass. This is a reminder that we have lost a little of our mindfulness because when we are properly in the present moment, we accept that everything is as it is, favourable or not. Impatience is a state of not accepting things as they are and not being able to deal with them with calmness and clarity. Each obstruction on the journey is a little lesson in cultivating what might be called natural patience; once we have cultivated it, there are no longer any obstructions.

- *Work and study*

If we see work as a chore, it means that we haven't yet developed the skill of mindfulness because we do not love what we do. When things are a chore, there is inevitably a feeling that we would rather be doing something else; part of us is missing to the extent that we cannot give our full presence, our full being, to what we are undertaking. Fulfilment is not possible under those circumstances and then we have a choice: to change ourselves or to change what we do. If we choose to change what we do, then the answer to dealing with things we would prefer not to deal with will always be to look for something else. Most of us have that habit already and it is one of the many forms of distraction and avoidance. The two extremes of this condition are the workaholic and the procrastinator. One seeks distraction by focusing on work to the exclusion of everything else; the other avoids issues by focusing on anything other than what needs to be dealt with. All of us probably have something of each trait in us and we also probably know that avoidance is not the answer.

The real answer is to love what we do. To love what we do, using the term literally rather than in its more familiar sense, means far more than enjoying what we do. After all, fulfilling a desire can be highly enjoyable but it doesn't necessarily mean that love is involved. To love what we do involves surrendering fully and giving fully – yin and yang in balance and totally satisfied. If, for example, someone loves gardening, they may say that when they are tending their plants they have a resonance in the heart – the heart almost "sings". Energy flows from their hands, giving them the euphemistic green fingers, their eyes sparkle and their skin is radiant; all this is because their inner self is finding expression in outer activity. But the same person may cringe at the prospect of housework, cooking a meal or washing up. That means that in those activities, as their enjoyment level takes a nosedive, the wonderful balance of yin and yang is gone. The previous level of energy isn't radiated at all and the connection with the soul – the inner connection – is temporarily lost.

Whether we work at home, in an office, a shop, a factory or in the open air; whether we have our own business or work for someone else; whether we are paid or are a volunteer; or are a student, carer or homemaker, doesn't matter – if we are to develop the qualities of the heart we must love what we do. To love what we do, we have to bring our full awareness into it so that the mind is not tempted to wander. We have to be like the gardener with green fingers. The major factor in cultivating this ability is acceptance – surrendering to the present. This isn't some ideological statement but is the only real practical and workable way of living. Surrendering to the present means that instead of internally fighting and objecting to whatever life brings to us, we simply accept that's the way things are and deal with them accordingly. So if there is a mess to clear up or a crisis to resolve, that's the way it is; there is a situation in which we need to act. We don't walk away but bring our full presence in and calmly face whatever is there. The gardener knows that there is more to gardening than admiring plants. Sometimes there is weeding to be done, flower beds to be prepared, the after-effects of storms or drought to be tackled and so on. Life is like that.

Bringing our awareness into work or study needs a little care. If we are enjoying what we do, it is possible to become too focused and forget to take a break. Our mind can be so tuned into the object of work – book, computer screen, machine, paperwork and so on – that it becomes a little closed and we develop a case of "mental tunnel vision". Awareness of our surroundings and of space is lost or restricted, resulting in a little tension that needs to be released. As a general rule, the human mind tends to focus on objects and not the space between objects. Yet the gap between objects is as important as the objects themselves in the same way that it is the relationship of notes to each other and to silence – the "space of sound" – that determines the quality of music.

At times in our work or study, if it is possible to do so, we should ease the mind by bringing our focus off the object of work and be aware of the space around us and our breath. We should smile and fill ourselves and our environment with love. Immediately there will be some relaxation and we will feel very good. The more often we can do this the better and our efficiency will increase as we bring more of our whole being into our work. Often we may be tempted to carry on – "I'll just finish this little bit," – and then we carry on and carry on without taking a break. This is where we need to take a little care and release the tension.

Constantly bringing our mind into the present moment, being aware of the space around us and not avoiding the things we don't like that nevertheless need our attention, we can fill our work with love and with a richness that no salary could ever match.

- *Listening and interacting*

Very few people really listen to what others say and yet it is one of the most wonderful gifts that one human being can give to another. It is also very difficult because even if we are paying full attention to what someone is talking about, the mind will often switch into calculating and anticipating mode, thinking how to respond or how what is being said applies to us. Perhaps one of the underlying reasons for this, apart from the natural tendency of the mind to wander, is the unconscious thought that the other person is separate from us. A product of viewing of things as separate, rather than as being magnificent wholeness, is that inevitably we will discriminate and prioritise; the need of the other person to be listened to is more likely than not to be lower down the list of priorities than our own perceived need to say something or to be somewhere else. There are exceptions, of course, and we are more likely to do a better job at listening to someone who is distraught than to something mundane.

The subject of listening is a vast one and there are techniques, such as active listening that counsellors are trained in, for example, that can be employed to ensure a greater engagement with someone who is speaking to us. Being mindful is another way and that means bringing our full awareness not only into what is being said but to the other person, to ourselves and to the space and relationship between us also.

There is something else we can do, too. Some people say this is very difficult and others say it is relatively easy. It requires use of the imagination, not to create something false, but to help correct our mistaken perception. It is to *see the other person as yourself*. What that means is to imagine that the person who is speaking to you *is* you. Without judgement, listen as though the speaker is a reflection of you. The effects of doing this can be amazing. Consciousness is listening to consciousness; consciousness is listening to itself. This is in fact a very deep truth. By using the imagination we temporarily suspend the belief in a separate "I"; the little self, the cause of all our problems, disappears for a while. Then we are truly able to listen.

Even if we find this is too hard or it makes us a little uncomfortable, we can simply take the approach that the other person is at this instant the most important person in the world. The speaking is happening now; if we listen with full awareness, there is communication and we live in the present moment; if we don't, we lose ourselves. The present moment is the only one there is and is the only time we can fully realise ourselves. When someone is talking to us, we have a choice: to be fully alive or to be partly dead. If we are fully alive, we will love that person in that moment. This is not the love of personal relationships, simply the love of life and everything that is. Through the ears and the eyes of listening, the fiery heart burns brightly and exudes great warmth.

- *And so to bed*

Whatever our activities have been during the day, finally the day ends and it is time to withdraw into a state of rest. Sleep is a time when, in effect, we should hand our body over in full trust and let nature perform its running repairs. Although we can survive with sleep deprivation, our better interests are served by ensuring so far as possible that we enjoy a good night's sleep. During the night, according to oriental medicine, various organs of the body go through cycles of activity and cleansing; resting helps those processes to take place and complete. The brain needs its rest, too, and there are many scientific studies on the benefits of sleep; indeed, there are institutions whose sole purpose is to increase the understanding of sleep and its effects.

The purpose of addressing sleep here is not so much to look at the benefits of sleep but to ensure that we approach it mindfully. One might be tempted to think that that is a little pointless because how can anyone be mindful about a state of unconsciousness? However, just as acting mindfully during the day enriches our experience of life no end, a mindful approach to night-time rest enriches the quality of sleep; more importantly, the combined result of both aspects enhances the overall state of consciousness and so our capacity for love.

Our night-time ablutions and undressing should be done with as much awareness and presence as getting ready in the mornings. That will be helped if we do not leave retiring until we are exhausted; we should feel pleasantly tired rather than drained. As with our space for meditation, where we sleep should be held as special and be respected. This will help to create the right atmosphere; a television or computer in the bedroom will detract from this, as will studying or reading in bed. If we live in one room, such as in a bedsit, or have to share a bedroom or sleep in a dormitory, we can still approach our own bed with reverence. It is not too much to say that the place where we sleep should be regarded in our own minds as a sacred spot. We can then get into bed with a calm and happy mind. If we are used to saying or thinking a prayer, particularly for the benefit of others, that also helps to produce a positive frame of mind.

Whether or not we do that (and it is something that can pay huge dividends in terms of developing our consciousness), before going to sleep it is useful to reflect on the day we have just lived. That reflection should only be on how *we* were, not on what we thought others did or didn't do. It need not be a long reflection – a minute or two will suffice – but it should be on the lines of thinking about the extent to which we were loving and selfless – or not – in thought, speech and action during the day. Having reflected, it is good to silently offer the whole day that is now ending. An offering can be to the highest expression of goodness we can think of according to our spiritual tradition or, if we have none, to humanity, the universe or to what I have called magnificent wholeness. The important thing is that the offering is made from the heart. Then we can lie resting with a light awareness on the breath or the body and allow sleep to come, as it surely will.

WE HAVE CHOICE

The little tips we have looked at in this chapter may strike a chord in you because they are all perfectly natural and lead to living more naturally. Outer life should be an expression of the inner life and living mindfully allows that to happen. It is not a process that should be forced – it is, after all, something that should be joyful – but at the same time it is necessary to invoke a little discipline, otherwise it will simply not be done. The mind will wander because that is what it has been doing in all of us throughout life so far, but with persistence it can be retrained. Some effort, therefore, is required but as soon as that effort is made, inner changes will be noticed.

To live mindfully requires a conscious decision. It won't happen by itself "one day". Once the decision is made, when do we begin? Not tomorrow, not even in a few minutes; we have to begin now, right this minute, right this second. Having begun, life immediately takes an upward turn. Bubbles of joy rise up from deep within us, at first at odd moments and then with increasing frequency; the elixir of love begins to ooze in the heart and the subtle pathways to bliss start to open in the body. Appreciation of life becomes stronger and then, at a point only known to the individual, it becomes possible to churn that elixir with some deeper practice and focus. This is what we will look at next.

7

THE PATH OF BLISS

A GREAT ACT OF COURAGE

Before bliss, comes courage. The word *courage* comes from the same root as the French word for heart – *coeur* – and at some point in everyone's spiritual journey there comes the realisation that the hardest yet most essential part of the path is to surrender oneself completely. To surrender everything one values for any cause takes the greatest courage and to do so for the highest good is a true act of the heart. The ultimate sacrifice is often a euphemism for giving up one's life and, both in modern times and throughout history, there have been countless great souls who have given up their lives for others. Almost certainly all of them at some instant before death inwardly surrendered themselves. In the evolution of the soul, this is of enormous significance.

Surrender is not an act reserved for life and death, though, but is an attitude that is relevant to the whole of life. Many people don't surrender with the heart but give things, activities or interests up because they think it is expected of them; they recognise that it is the right thing to do rather than it being something they want to do. Most of us are probably like that to at least some degree, for it is a rare person indeed who is attached to nothing at all. But spiritual surrender means giving up oneself entirely, inwardly the greatest sacrifice we can make.

On our spiritual path of fully expressing the inner self through the development of love, the surrendering of the self is normally a gradual process. So far we have been considering important, but nevertheless gentle, methods of unfolding the heart. If followed, they will make huge differences to life. They will generate sufficient warmth in the heart so that there will soon be the beginnings of spiritual fire. However, we can do more. We can intensify the heat so that it burns all the dross left by the ego in a process of mental purification. To do this doesn't require great intellectual power or stamina but it does require constant effort. The rewards of doing this are immense, for the result at some point will be to generate bliss.

Bliss comes when the heart is fully open, because then the flow of energy is very strong. When we are at our most generous, we give love not only outwards into our environment but inwards and upwards also. From within us comes a great outpouring of energy – not physical energy, although that may well be heightened, but energy of a spiritual kind. Furthermore, the opening of this amazing, dynamic centre of the heart also allows energy to come *into* us as the whole being becomes more receptive to love of a higher kind. In effect, a communication takes place, an interchange of energy that creates a thrill throughout our whole being.

This thrill is bliss. Bliss is not the aim of our practice because if it were we would become attached to it and so become stuck in a type of spiritual materialism; it is a by-product, something that happens as we lose our inhibitions about the divine and see that what I have called *magnificent wholeness* is real, is conscious and intelligent. This is why this chapter is entitled *The Path of Bliss* and not *The Path to Bliss.* Bliss is part of the scenery on the way but is not the destination. If we remember this, we will keep to the right path.

Over the following pages, we are going to look at love of a very deep and special nature. Unless we have been brought up and have lived in a certain way, we may find that there is resistance in us to this path and we should not take it, perhaps, unless we feel ready. On the other hand, resistance often prevents us from taking opportunities when they arise and so we lose out. All that is asked of you now is that if you read these pages, please do so with an open mind. For some people this path is easy but for many it takes time and a great deal of effort to adjust. It is very common for much thought and reasoning to have been given or applied to spiritual matters, without much feeling from the heart. This is normal. We are not going to throw out logic with the baby and the bathwater because what follows is entirely logical – however it may not seem so if our logic is blinkered and narrow. The idea is not to sacrifice the head of reason in the fires of the heart but to bring head and heart together, properly balanced and blended.

THE SOURCE OF LOVE

Love is divine. It may be an old adage but it is not very difficult to see that it is absolutely true. The divine is synonymous with the highest good imaginable and love is the highest or purest expression of goodness which we can be aware of or can imagine. Whether we want to use the term God to describe the divine or prefer some other expression is neither here nor there; the fact remains that true love is very sincere, very pure and of ineffable goodness. From our human experience, we know that some people feel or express love more than others and we also know that an individual can love less in some instances and more in others. Love is not finite, therefore; it is variable according to one's state of consciousness in any given moment. Love is an expression of consciousness itself and, as the potential for consciousness is limitless, so is that for love.

To cope with the enormity of higher expressions of love, all cultures have described divine personalities so that the human mind can relate in some way to the divine or the sacred. Christ, Kuan Yin, Divine Mother, Earth Mother, Devi, the Buddha, Tara and hundreds if not thousands more names and descriptions of sources of divine love and compassion exist, each exemplifying an extraordinary state of consciousness that expresses a love so powerful and all-encompassing that the human mind cannot take it in – but can imagine it at least a little.

A symptom of this secular age is that many minds are closed to the possibility of the divine or to the possible existence of beings with higher, all-embracing states of consciousness. They think there is nothing after death, that consciousness is a mere product of the physical body and brain and that the only intelligent life is that which exists on planet Earth. This is not the place to go into an argument about that type of thinking except to say that any individual consciousness that denies the possibility of higher states of consciousness also denies itself. Consciousness by its very nature cannot be finite, nor can love. The rejection of religion by the majority of people in our society (there are very notable exceptions but the demise of churches in many communities makes it very evident) may be due in part to the insistence of religious leaders on adherence to blind faith rather than allowing an intelligent inquiry. Sadly, this rejection has also led to an emphasis on worldly values and to a form of spiritual amnesia. In turn, this has resulted in a very restricted view of life which sees humanity and its world as the be-all-and-end-all of everything. This is changing very slowly; science is beginning to see much deeper values – and mysteries – about life and our universe (even if humanity is, as yet, still seen as the only intelligent life) and many people are yearning to express their inner nature, intuiting that there is something more than the mundane – something within them that is waiting to flourish.

In our quest for meaning in life, one thing becomes very clear – nothing is isolated and totally independent. At the end of chapter 5, we touched on the idea of magnificent wholeness and it would be helpful to consider that a little more. If we look at any object, it has the appearance of an object but a deeper scrutiny reveals that nothing is quite what it seems. A tree can be called a tree because it has a trunk and branches; it also has roots and either leaves or needles. Yet if a branch is broken off, the tree is still a tree. When the leaves fall or when the needles shed, there is still a tree. But when it is felled, there is no longer a tree. There will be a stump in the ground and timber lying nearby before being carted away. The ingredients or parts that made up the tree, its components, still exist but the tree is no more. Our use of the word *tree* is simply a way of labelling an appearance or a form. The timber may be made into furniture or a shed and the leaves and smaller branches may be macerated into mulch. Nothing has disappeared from the planet – the collection of matter that was labelled a tree has merely changed. And when did the tree become a tree? At one point there was a seed and from the seed a shoot sprouted. Later on there was a sapling but on what date did it stop being a sapling and become a tree? The tree was never born or created; it evolved. When we look at how it evolved, in addition to the seed there was the requirement of the correct conditions and so earth, light, warmth, moisture, air and space were all necessary. None of these contributory conditions is isolated and independent. Each has its complex causes and none of them can be nailed down as having a permanent, independent nature.

Everything is tied up with everything else and so everything is part of "the else of everything else". The lack of an independent nature was described by one of the world's great teachers, the Buddha, as *emptiness.*[22] Some people have latched onto that word as meaning a void or a vacuum,

---

22 The *Prajnaparamita Diamond Sutra.* See, for example, *The Diamond That Cuts Through Illusion,* Thich Nhat Hanh, Parallax Press 1992.

implying that nothing exists, which was not what was meant at all. For that reason, it is probably easier for us to think of everything as being an appearance or an aspect of *wholeness*. An analogy is that there are waves on the ocean that can be ripples, swell, huge breakers that are the dream of surfers or even a tsunami, but all are simply appearances of water or ocean. They do not have a separate, permanent existence in their own right.

The purpose of looking down this road for a few moments is to make it clear that love is not something that originates with us as individuals because, in effect, we don't originate anything. Everything arises because of a multiplicity of conditions. The wave does not originate the white spume that may adorn it as a crest in wild weather, nor does it originate the refreshing coolness that soothes the bather in the heat of summer. These qualities occur because of other factors. Similarly, love arises from our inherent nature as a result of conscious awareness. There has to be an awareness of something and there also has to be the quality of love arising from within consciousness.

The source of love might therefore be said to be consciousness itself. We as individuals are like anything else in the universe – we appear but a permanent, separate and independent true nature cannot be found because we are made up of components and causes. Like the reality of the waves is water, our reality is magnificent wholeness but we are only capable of expressing a minuscule speck of its potential. As our consciousness evolves, we are able to express deeper and more wholesome qualities. At first we may hardly express these qualities, if we express them at all, but little by little they progressively manifest, so becoming a real part of us. The process of evolution of consciousness is one of realisation – making its inherent qualities a reality that is experienced and lived. Reading about love or any other aspect of consciousness means nothing until it is realised, in the same way that reading recipes in a cookery book doesn't transform us into cooks or produce the slightest morsel of food. The experience has to be real.

Now, if love is an aspect of magnificent wholeness, it is a quality that can manifest anywhere, given the right conditions. It also follows that there can be no limit to the strength or extent of love – limits cannot be imposed on the boundless nor can the infinite be made finite. That means that the expression of love is limited only by the consciousness of that which loves. So we have, in a sense, two parallel considerations. One is that love is expressed by consciousness which itself is an aspect of magnificent wholeness; the other is that love is only limited by the consciousness or capacity of the being or entity that expresses it. Therefore we have what might be termed the *original source* of love – wholeness – and there is an infinite range of capacities for expressing it.

The original source is that which is and encompasses everything – some call this God, some call it the Absolute, others call it the Self, some the Divine Mother, others the Divine Father, the Great White Spirit and hundreds if not thousands of other names. In this book I have used the term magnificent wholeness because for many people anything that sounds as though it could possibly have religious connotations causes walls of resistance to spring up. That would be a shame and a waste. Never mind that for now – the important thing is to understand that the universe is not empty space with a few bright lights and rocks in it. Our universe is wonderfully alive; if it weren't, we couldn't be either.

GREATER EXPRESSIONS OF LOVE

Is it possible that there are beings of far greater consciousness than the human and who are capable of expressing love? Perhaps the phrase "is it possible" is a little inapt because either there are or there are not. However, the human mind has great ability in limiting its view to what it believes. Some people are adamant that there is nothing beyond human life – what you see is what you get. WYSIWYGs have a belief system based not on proof that there is nothing but rather on the absence of any proof that there is anything else. Then there are the theists – those who believe there is God, or perhaps a multiplicity of gods, and whose beliefs vary enormously from that of a Creator to an impersonal God and to those where there are myriad gods, each representing different characteristics or impulses of natural law. Some people prefer to be open-minded, others believe in life going on and evolving after death, others still are certain that there are various beings that control all our destinies.

No-one can be absolutely sure of anything that they have not experienced but there are intuitive states of mind in which wider and even abstract concepts can be grasped when the mind has become sufficiently calm and clear. It is a little like being in a dimly lit room that one has become accustomed to through years of living in it when one day it is discovered that part of one of the walls isn't a wall at all but is a curtain that can be drawn back. Suddenly the room looks rather different as daylight sweeps into it and, looking at the source of light, a much bigger world can be seen. So it is that occasionally, usually after much meditative experience, a different world of reality, one that is far more expansive than that we are used to, is detected, albeit vaguely at first. Then it becomes apparent that not only are we not the highest expressions of consciousness, but that we are surrounded by sources of extraordinary intelligence and love, far greater than the human mind can comprehend.

If such an experience happens, it will be an intuitive one in which there is no need for the intellect to label things as this or that. There will be no need or desire to tell others because that is a trait of the lower mind and of the ego. It is the ego that makes people want to boast of their special experience or of "having seen the light". It is a quiet experience, perhaps accompanied by bliss or more often simply a realisation of being surrounded by extraordinary goodness. It is at once both amazing and blindingly obvious. This new vista in our awareness can arise only innocently. If we try to contrive it, the reality we perceive will also be contrived, like flowers made of silk which may have a fine appearance but are not flowers. There are many people who portray themselves as purveyors of spirituality in this so-called new age but who are nothing more than merchants of fancy silk.

We should rightly be cautious of all marketing of enlightenment and of self-styled saviours. Your spirituality and mine is not to be found elsewhere but is already within us. The curtains that keep the light out are of our own making and we simply have to draw them open. As the intuition dawns, we will know that for certain. We will also know that love is a certainty and that humanity does not possess the sole rights to deal in it; it is universal.

That there are beings we cannot see with our physical eyes expressing great love is something we can imagine, even if we haven't yet developed much of an intuitive sense. To deny that they might exist and assert that the only source of love can be God is a little like saying that there can be only one source of heat and light – the sun – when we know that the sun's light and heat is transmitted to us in countless ways. Even our own body heat has its origins in the sun; and just as a forest fire and a light bulb both manifest heat in different ways, so love can be expressed in great and small ways. The point, really, though, is this: does it make any difference to us if we know, believe or imagine that there are expressions or manifestations of consciousness greater than the human? The answer is that it opens up a vast potential in us; if our mind is open to all possibilities, then all things become possible. It is one of the oldest maxims of creativity. In our theme of developing love, opening to all possibilities will immediately increase our potential because our ability to love is limited only by the mind and by the emotions. We will return to this opening up shortly. First, let us consider a form of love that is so intense and powerful that it can dissolve all hardness and resistance, like a laser that can cut through any obstacle.

THE GREATEST FORM OF LOVE

Love is difficult because it entails giving up all self-interest and so the majority of us are fairly amateurish in our approach. Most of the time, our love is more watery than fiery. Love for family and friends may vary from a more intense love for a life-partner to one that is considerably less so for friends. It isn't wrong to be like this – it is the normal human reaction to other people that depends on so many things that colour our perceptions – but we can do better. Love for people is also difficult at times because we tend to see the personalities rather than the true nature that underlies them. Without loving people any less – indeed the opposite is likely to be true – it is possible to learn to love the divine and in doing so cause our heart to overflow. This can be developed to such a degree of strength that it can cause the hair to stand up on the back of the neck and make the eyes run with tears; when it flows abundantly, the elixir of the heart fills the body with bliss.

Love of such strength is called devotion and it takes effort and practice for it to develop. Why should we want to develop it? Because it has the capacity to lift us out of all suffering and ignorance and to transform us into spiritual beings. The bliss of devotion raises the vibration of the mind and the body; the mundane events in life no longer hold us down. The eyes see with a different vision, the ears hear that which needs to be heard and the tongue utters only positive, uplifting and appropriate speech. All these things and much more are possible when the heart is transformed through devotion.

Devotion might be thought of as a false state that causes a person to become a little strange and other-worldly. After all, does it not make a person lose all touch with reality? Is it not devotion that causes people to beat tambourines, knock at doors proselytising or go round city streets chanting mantras? Maybe so but that is not the type of devotion that is being described here. This devotion is a very private affair because the heart is a private matter. You cannot develop strong arms by telling other people how much weight you can lift nor can you run fast by boasting what a good sprinter you are. Those who practise devotion outwardly must perfect it inwardly first, otherwise their words and actions will be empty.

True love involves surrender and so it follows that total love means total surrender. Devotion is nothing more than total love that is focused and, in order that it is kept free of the impurities of the lower mind, the strongest and most powerful way is to train our devotion on the divine or something that represents the divine to us. To do so fully means surrendering one's entire self to the divine or to the highest principle we can envisage. One surrenders, in effect, to the source of love. As love is the purest quality we can express, we offer the purest aspect of our nature to the purest aspect of the universe we can imagine. When we think of it in those terms, devotion is no longer the prerogative of the oddball but is actually the highest expression of a human being. Inevitably, it will bring out the best qualities of the individual; inevitably, it also takes a long time to perfect – if, indeed, it can be perfected.

Surrendering the highest aspect of oneself to the highest aspect of the universe doesn't sound quite so bad now, does it? But thinking it is a good idea and actually doing it are, of course, two different things. We will all have reservations and, no matter with what good intent we may start, there will be times when we make excuses or prefer to forget the idea altogether. Human beings are full of "yes, buts" and never more strongly than when we are being invited to step out of our comfort zones. But if we never step out of those zones, we will never move and will never change; then one day it will be time to die and we might wonder, rather belatedly, what life was actually for. On the other hand, the present moment is an ever-present opportunity for change and spiritual growth. Transforming life into bliss *is* possible and we can begin that transformation now. As with many things, it is better to do it in stages and the first of those is simply to open to the divine.

OPENING TO THE DIVINE

Opening to the divine requires two things; one is allowing our awareness to expand and the other is acceptance. Expanding our awareness brings about a certain broadening of vision or perception and isn't something that involves any technical or sophisticated application. The problem with awareness in a busy world is that it is restricted and somewhat narrow. Our focus is on objects rather than the space between them, on sounds and noise rather than the silence in which they arise and on concepts and beliefs rather than on freedom from thought. As a result, the mind is busy leaping from one thing to another or going round in circles, repeating patterns of thought. Many people are uncomfortable sitting in silence and require distractions or entertainment lest they drown in the void of their own being. Yet what we need to do, most of us, is learn the ability to enjoy silence and our own company so that the mind becomes freer. If we meditate already, we will have some idea about how to do this but if we don't, it will pay us great dividends to learn to sit quietly. All we need to do is sit in an upright but comfortable position, place the awareness on the gentle movement of the breath and close the eyes. Having the awareness in the abdomen, just below the navel, is helpful while doing this. The rhythm of the breath will be felt there and bringing the awareness to this part of the body helps to slow the mind down. Ten minutes of sitting quietly like this will relax the mind and the body greatly and a sense of ease will gradually come.

This relaxation is very important as it is virtually impossible to be open to the world around us and to the divine when the mind is tense. Having established some sense of ease, it is good to look around and appreciate our surroundings, no matter what they are. We should do this without judgement and it is particularly helpful if we maintain a sense of space rather than feeling we are surrounded by objects or walls. Gradually the mind will become easier and more comfortable. Then we can simply consider, without too much thought, that everything is an expression of the divine, of God, of magnificent wholeness or whatever term we are happy with.

It is not much of a step then to accept things as they are. Everything is as it is. All appearances arise in our consciousness because of conditions coming together now, so we can just accept the present as it is. Acceptance means that we do not fight the present moment nor do we judge it; it just is. That doesn't imply that things that need changing shouldn't be changed; in every moment we are creating conditions that affect the future and the whole universe is governed by the law of cause and effect. For now, we can safely embrace the present moment because there is no other moment in which we can be and this acceptance means that we also embrace magnificent wholeness which in itself is divine expression. Notice that by using the word *embrace*, accepting has a hint of warmth about it. Some people regard acceptance as being an act of putting up with something because there is no other option; here it is meant in the sense of a welcoming acceptance, as one would a new friend, work colleague or member of a family. If we welcome and accept each moment and everything in each moment, we are not far from learning to love the divine.

It is true that love expands our consciousness but it is also the case that our consciousness or awareness needs to expand in order to love. In order to love, there has to be a link in our consciousness to someone or something. It is impossible to love nothing. So to love someone we need to be aware of them and to love the divine we need to be aware of the divine. For many people the divine is something abstract, just an idea of something incomprehensible, and that makes loving the divine very difficult. To use another analogy, the atmosphere of this world is full of radio signals of all types but we cannot become aware of them, let alone make any sense of them, unless we tune in with the right apparatus. The divine is a little bit like that – we need to tune in otherwise we cannot see or hear anything. If we cannot love without tuning in, we certainly cannot generate devotion without doing so.

Devotion carries with it the sweetest and strongest form of bliss and although everyone would like that very much, few are willing to do what is necessary to transform their lives from a mundane, and sometimes stressed, existence into a blissful state. The bliss of loving the divine is available to everyone and it doesn't involve leading a religious or fanatical life, nor does it mean that all common sense has to be sacrificed. On the contrary, once we start to tune in, we soon realise that a huge part of our real self is opening up to us and that the divine is not the domain of religion at all; it is within every living creature. Moreover, as the divine is supremely intelligent and is the source of all intelligence, we make greater contact with our own inner intelligence. If we deny the divine, we are also denying ourselves. It is a bit like a person living in the back-of-beyond denying there is such a thing as television because they have never seen a television set or disbelieving that it is possible to have a conversation with someone on the other side of the world. Such disbelief is understandable but is also based in ignorance.

The problem for many in approaching this subject is how to focus on the divine. How do we learn to love the divine if the divine encompasses everything in the universe? If the divine is transcendent in nature and formless, how can one focus on something that has no form?

There are a number of possible approaches – and there need to be because each one of us is different. Let's remember first of all that the divine is intelligent and is the source of everything because it *is* everything. All intelligence that any creature has can only come from the overall field of intelligence and all love springs from the same source. By definition, the divine – magnificent wholeness – must be omniscient; if it isn't, there is no divine. The divine therefore knows itself and all appearances in our universe are therefore known to the divine. Its limitless intelligence means that it has the capacity to communicate in any form that is appropriate. If it couldn't, it would be limited not limitless. So we have choice. In whatever way we wish to communicate or link with the divine, we may do so; if we choose not to, that's fine but we remain closed off. For some, it is relatively easy to imagine the divine as manifesting, for example, as a spiritual teacher or a deity of some description. As long as the individual does not see that personification as the *only* divine manifestation, this is a very useful way of focusing the mind. Devotion is easier when we see the divine as real, receptive and communicative. Using the imagination to visualise the divine can be a very powerful way of expanding and extending one's consciousness and can break down many internal barriers that prevent or hinder the enlightenment process. Even if we are not used to visualising, it is a method that can be extraordinarily fruitful, even for those who think they are too intelligent to do such things.

However, seeing or visualising a form is not imperative. There is little doubt that the divine has the attributes of both form and formlessness. The important thing is to think of the divine as intelligent, loving and receptive, which it most certainly is. Suppose you are composing a letter or an email to someone you haven't actually met and have no idea what they look like. It is still possible for you to communicate. Correspondence may even pass between you so that some sort of rapport builds up between you. Gradually a relationship of sorts develops – perhaps an air of friendliness and trust. You have probably experienced such things but even if you haven't, it is not so hard to imagine them as possible.

Whichever way we choose, it is important to build up a relationship in our minds with the divine. As we become used to communicating, whether through prayer or through addressing our thoughts and feelings (which is a form of prayer), we will gradually establish a rapport. Divine intelligence is not deaf; it will pick up on our thoughts. Like a listener who is very wise, loving and compassionate, the divine absorbs what we are saying and will respond – not as a disembodied voice from the sky, but with energy that is supportive and wholly appropriate for our needs. The closer we can draw to that divine source, the more easily and readily we will benefit. How do we draw closer? By trusting the divine and learning to love. When we are able to have that trust, we are like a plant that draws water and nutrients from the soil in which it grows. Learning to love the divine makes us flourish. If we don't have that trust, the growth of our spirituality will be stunted and will eventually wither.

DEVOTION

Once we begin to establish this relationship, the path to devotion is not far. Devotion means making the relationship special and the most effective way to achieve this is through sincere communication or prayer. Prayer is simply expressing our innermost thoughts and there are many ways of doing that; it may be through thoughts, words or action but the important thing is to do it with the heart. Gradually we will learn to surrender the ego – the little self that noisily makes itself heard with its judgements, its pettiness and selfishness. Devotion means offering our whole self; it is a surrender of everything we may regard as personal to us – all our self-interests, fears and desires – but not in a painful or unpleasant way. The ego will resist and object to any thought of surrender but it is just like a wave on the sea of the divine. Once the wave knows it is water, it can relax as water, whatever its form. Until then, the ego struggles to preserve itself and inevitably suffers.

It is important that our relationship with the divine is a joyful one, otherwise how can bliss come? The process starts slowly and at times will inevitably falter. One thing we can do is actually ask for help in generating devotion, in developing a heart that is filled with love, not only for the divine but for ourselves and our fellow human beings also. It takes courage to ask because this is an area of resistance in most of us; but once that resistance is dissolved, a wonderful form of energy flows through us.

In practising devotion, it is vital that we live normally and do not cut ourselves off from the world. We should still read, inquire and reflect. If we work, we should still work; if we look after a home, we should still do so. In fact, we should do all that we do now but with more enthusiasm, unless we know it is harmful, of course. Love for our family, friends and other loved ones should increase immeasurably as we become more in touch with the universal source of love. Sometimes we will experience bliss and there will also be periods, sometimes lengthy, when bliss seems to have deserted us. That is fine; bliss is unimportant. What is essential is the development of love – the elixir of the heart.

8

INTELLIGENCE, ENGINEERING, MAGNETISM AND GLUE

Within and throughout the entire universe, there is something that holds everything together. For some mysterious reason, forces contrive to keep things in their place. Planets maintain their various orbits round the sun, solar systems have their positions relative to each other, some in patterns as constellations, and there are the tremendous collections of heavenly bodies we call galaxies. Gazing up at a star-filled sky on a clear night can have a wonderful effect on the mind. The enormity of it all is extraordinary; the beauty stunning and the distances almost beyond comprehension. Who has never been impressed by such a sight?

That the universe is structured, there is no doubt. Galaxies and the solar systems within them form coherent masses of matter. If they were not structured and balanced, everything would disintegrate. There has to be within the entire universe a force that holds things together, a natural or universal law, which applies everywhere. That means in turn that the universe is organised somehow – not from outside but from within itself. It responds to organising power and there are "rules" to which the whole responds. The law of attraction or magnetism is one of these rules. Like yin and yang, there has to be an opposing force otherwise everything would collapse in on itself; so there has to be another natural law – repulsion – to allow coherence and structure. We could say that magnetism is yin and repulsion is yang; both must be balanced for there to be harmony. There are many other rules or natural laws. The law of cause and effect is one and mutual interdependence is another, as is impermanence or the inevitability of change.

So far as the structure of the human body is concerned, similar principles apply as to celestial bodies. Both macrocosm and microcosm subsist while the law of magnetism holds things together. Each cell in the body is like a miniature solar system, with a nucleus and its surrounding material which maintains a relationship with it, and some organising intelligence holding the whole structure of the body together. Science has located that intelligence as being in the DNA – but intelligence itself is invisible, as indeed is love. The reproduction of bodies, too, relies on attraction or magnetism of the sexes and so the principle goes on. That physical bodies and objects require a cohesive force is not difficult to see or understand.

The universe that we know as the physical universe is only that which is detectable or discernible because it is within a certain range of perception. We can only perceive those things that are within the range of our senses and can only detect that which is within the range of instruments available to us. For example, we cannot see or hear radio waves but we can do so when they have been reduced and transformed through receiving apparatus to a frequency that the ear can detect or the eyes can see. This is an oversimplification but it is the overall principle that is important, pointing to matter that cannot be detected because its frequency is beyond the scope of instruments, as well as to much finer levels of the universe which are of too high a wavelength to be seen or detected.

Those who have had experience of meditation over a period of time know that the hearing, sight and other senses gradually become more refined as we become used to different states of consciousness. Similarly, those who practise the healing arts or who work with energy become more aware of finer levels of energy. Ironically, acupuncture is available in many areas under the National Health Service but science says, for the moment at least, that the meridians do not exist because they cannot be detected or measured. If there are finer energy pathways within the human organism that are beyond the scope of scientific instruments, there must also be energy pathways within the cosmos that cannot as yet be detected. As is the case with the human organism, there is more to the cosmos than the eye can see or the instrument can measure or detect.

The human being can, through training, attain more coherent states of consciousness and we know that the experiences of a meditator, for example, are reflected to some degree in the physical body. The breathing and heart rates slow down, the blood pressure drops and, interestingly, the wave patterns created by the brain (as recorded on an electro-encephalograph) become more coherent. As a general rule, a person who meditates on a regular basis enjoys better health than would otherwise be the case because the immune system is stronger and the body ages at a slower rate.[23] Such physical effects, which are measurable, arise from a state of consciousness that is not measurable. Simply by taking the awareness into deeper levels of consciousness, greater orderliness takes place at the physical level. In other words an "engineering effect", an effect on the physical structure and its maintenance, occurs as a result of consciousness. The physical structure is made more orderly by something deeper than itself, some innate intelligence.

If this is the case in the microcosm of the human being, it follows that there is a high possibility of innate intelligence within other microcosms and within the macrocosm of the universe itself. If the experience of the meditator were a fluke, such physical responses would not arise generally in those who meditate, but they do. That means there is a law at work and where there is a law, it likely occurs elsewhere. That in turn would mean there has to be intelligence or orderliness underlying everything and there have to be subtler levels of awareness and activity, not just for human beings but throughout the universe. But that intelligence would not be able to come from a Creator pulling strings

---

23 There has been considerable research on this. See, for example, *Transcendental Meditation, mindfulness, and longevity: an experimental study with the elderly*, Alexander, Langer, Newman, Chandler and Davies, Journal of Personality and Social Psychology 1989.

like a magnificent puppeteer; it would have to be inherent within the universe itself.

Somehow we have to understand that the outer appearance, i.e. the physical structure, of the universe, reflects or responds to its inner intelligence. In the same way that the form of your body and mine supports and provides conditions for experience of consciousness or inner intelligence, in some unfathomable way the stars, galaxies and the whole cosmos have to be governed by inner intelligence and serve it by providing a vehicle for consciousness. That doesn't mean to say that everything is conscious in the same way that we are conscious; after all, the physical anatomy of our bodies is not the same as our consciousness. For instance, our toenails help provide part of the body as a structure for the expression of consciousness but do not, so far as we know, have the capacity for thought. Nevertheless, toenails would not have come into being were there not a need for a physical structure. Similarly, perhaps the physical structures within the universe, the planets and moons that appear to us to be lifeless, came into being as part of or as a result of a vast unfolding of intelligence or consciousness, albeit totally beyond our comprehension. In other words, the physical universe and the structures within it are a collection of vehicles for the expression of consciousness. The "cosmic glue" that binds the universe together – the invisible magnetism – must also be a result of that expression and there is a correlation between it and what we know as love.

We know from personal experience that the inner affects the outer. How our mind is, both in thoughts and in the attitudes that colour them, affects our speech and our actions. If we are happy, how we interact with others and with the world around us is entirely different to when we are sad or angry. Our outer life reflects our inner state. Although we may often put things down to chance or luck, in the main our personal circumstances are the result of our inner processes coupled with the inner processes of other people. Families, for example, don't just happen by accident; at some point, two people are drawn to each other by desire and children are conceived as a result of desire. Whether we have a trade, profession or calling, look after a home or take a job for the simple reason of earning a living, to have an occupation requires us to have made a decision or a number of decisions either to enter into it or into a chain of events that resulted in it. Likes, dislikes, desires and beliefs produce the way we are; we reject this and pursue that and the events of life are coloured by our thoughts, emotions and perceptions.

Of all the qualities that affect or colour our consciousness, love is by far the strongest and the most long-lasting. Love unites; it bridges the gaps in our awareness and it shapes our lives. Love, as we can experience it and understand it, is the most sublime form of magnetism. It brings living beings together and it brings out the finest spiritual qualities. Love has the potential, as we saw in the last chapter, to generate bliss. As that which we call the divine must also love, does it not make sense that the love of the divine, so majestic and enormous that a human mind couldn't begin to contemplate it, is the inner cause of the law of magnetism that brings and holds everything together? Whatever mess our minds make of things, our true role is to perfect the expression of love in our own lives. Then we will fulfil our potential – the microcosm expressing the intention of the macrocosm. How else can divine intention be played out than by every unit of consciousness realising itself and realising its potential? As is famously said, its roots needs must be in mud but the full beauty of the lotus is not fully known until the flower blooms. Every human being is like the lotus; our history and experience are our roots and our hearts are like lotus buds waiting to open. When they do, the result will be the most beautiful expression of consciousness imaginable.

THE WORLD MUST CHANGE – AND LOVE IS THE KEY

Is it possible for the world to change for the better? It is easy to become despondent about the state of many things in the world of humanity and we have to be careful not to do that, otherwise we will develop a negative mind. This era we are in, when spiritual values seem to be diminishing by the day, has long been prophesied. *Kali yuga* – the age of darkness or ignorance – is foretold in many of the eastern scriptures and classical texts. But the good news is that *kali yuga* is said to be just one of a cycle of ages and from it knowledge, goodness and enlightenment eventually emerge.

Another thing to cheer us is that the problems of humanity, aside from those caused by natural disasters, arise from errors in human consciousness and so can be rectified. Humanity's challenge is not so much to change outer circumstances but to change inner consciousness; then the necessary outer changes will naturally follow. The fundamental error in consciousness is the blindness or ignorance of seeing ourselves as separate from everyone and everything else. This view of separateness results in a tendency to divisiveness in human affairs. The individual is concerned with his or her own interests above everyone else's and groups of individuals are concerned primarily with their own group's interests or purposes, whether that group is a family, a community, a nation, a race, a religion or a commercial concern. Affairs at every level of society are therefore coloured by self-interest. That is naturally divisive and inevitably causes imbalance in society, and unnecessary suffering.

The problems of humanity are very complex but the antidote is simple. To repair cracks, glue is needed and the cracks in consciousness can be repaired with cosmic glue – not the force that holds the planets and solar systems together but the glue of consciousness that this book is about: love. Love is unifying in every way – it brings people together, increases understanding and will eventually bring nations together. But it has to manifest in the individual; the problems of the world will only be solved when each of us learns to love. That requires some focused self-improvement.

IMPROVING SELF, IMPROVING WORLD

Never is there a moment in life when it is not possible to practise some form of self-improvement. The difficulty is recognising what can be done and then applying sufficient will and energy to do it. Before we look at this in a little more detail, it might be useful to think about what self-improvement really is.

From a material point of view it is easy to understand that self-improvement might involve altering those circumstances in life that affect material comfort or perhaps status. Certainly the young are conditioned by education and parenting to recognize that work brings material rewards in terms of standards of living. It would be wrong to ignore this area of life but, like many things, if the focus is entirely on one aspect, imbalance occurs. Sadly, the West has become driven largely by the work ethic and has lost many values in the process. Even the welfare principle behind social security, originally introduced to alleviate poverty, has suffered as more and more people seek rewards and rights for themselves that go beyond needed assistance. By and large, the focus of the majority of individuals is not so much on what improvements they could make to the world around them but what they can draw on to benefit their own personal circumstances.

But if we turn that around just a little and think of how we can improve ourselves so that we react in a way that is beneficial to the wider environment, the focus changes. Instead of thinking of our own comfort and wanting things for ourselves, we begin to see how we affect others by our thinking, by our speech and by our reactions to all events in life. Instead of seeing the world as a resource to draw upon, we see it as both a learning environment and one to which we may contribute. Looking at things from this perspective, it is not so difficult to see that life is an enormous opportunity. We can, if we choose, pass it up or ignore it; alternatively we can grasp it with both hands and improve ourselves and our world simultaneously.

From this point of view, education has a vast role to play and many educationalists are philanthropists also. The problem for us is that once school, college or university is over, education in any formal sense tends to stop. Then we rely on, or are subject to, the media or our own voluntary inquiry for information that can transform the way we think. If we tackle this responsibly, we can make steady and sometimes significant inroads; but if we are to transform ourselves into better and more responsible human beings, there has to be an inner change that does not depend just on intellectual understanding. Intellectual understanding is important but it doesn't necessarily make us into kinder, more compassionate or more selfless human beings. Something in us has to transcend the tendency to want things for ourselves and instead see very clearly that we are all part of one magnificent whole.

Such changes occur, generally speaking, over a long

period of time. Only occasionally do we receive a clear glimpse of things as they really are so that our internal reactions to outer events alter in any significant way. We are, after all, creatures of habit and will only change our habits with focused effort. Fortunately, the habits that are most important are those of the mind – the way we tend to think – and the mind is flexible, albeit it with a tendency to be obstinate.

While it is important to understand the issues affecting the world or our wider environment, the most major contribution we can make is through retraining the mind so that our approach to it changes. If the way we react to the world changes from the inside, the outer responses we make through our actions and our words will have an increasing tendency to be life-supporting and will create an atmosphere of harmlessness around us. All wars and all conflict, which are the cause of so much suffering, are not caused by nature but arise because of the internal reactions of human beings to outer circumstances – nothing else. Peace must arise inwardly before it can be manifested outwardly.

How can we create the circumstances or conditions that will enable us to use every moment in life as an opportunity for self-improvement in this way? So many people think that they will only be able to do something of this nature later on when they have more time – when their studies have finished or they have a better job, when the children have left school or home, or when they have retired or no longer have to look after ageing relatives. The bad news is that the extra time we think will come probably won't because there is always something that needs to be done.

Even when we die, the in-tray is still not empty. However, the much better news is that it is not extra time that is needed for self-improvement but a change in approach to every second of the day. Then we may see that there is no future to wait for; there is only the present, a time to be revered and cherished.

The key to improving our internal reactions is to be aware of them rather than responding automatically to them. Suppose, for example, that someone says something that makes us angry. Habitual reactions may normally make us respond in an angry way, either through words spoken angrily or through a physical reaction such as storming out of the room and slamming the door. Feelings of anger are unpleasant enough and if we respond with anger, we only increase our inner discomfort as well as creating unpleasantness in the atmosphere. But if we can maintain sufficient presence of mind to recognise and acknowledge the feelings within us rather than respond emotionally, there is a very good chance of dealing with both the situation and ourselves in a more enlightened fashion.

Our internal reactions are governed by two elements: our emotional make-up and our habitual patterns of thought. These have innumerable causative conditions that are extraordinarily complex and are different for every individual. It would be impossible, and probably not very fruitful, to examine them all. The important point is that self-improvement is about re-educating oneself in the here-and-now. One of the most effective methods is to bring our full awareness not only into *what* we are doing, but also into *how* we are doing it.

To be aware of our feelings while we are doing things might seem impractical and also rather self-indulgent. At first, perhaps, it is better just to bring our full awareness into the activity we are doing. If we are washing a mug and plate, for example, we should bring our full awareness into washing them carefully and not think about other things. For most of us, simply acting mindfully will be a major advancement and will significantly help us to achieve a greater clarity of mind. At a slightly deeper level, we can also be aware of our feelings. For life to be enjoyed, our feelings should be positive but sometimes they are negative in nature, sometimes they are overrun by desire and, at other times, they can be completely neutral or flat.

The Buddha taught that by being aware of our breathing we become more aware of our body and, by bringing awareness and therefore greater stillness into our body, we can also be more aware of our feelings, our thought patterns and our perceptions. When feelings arise, rather than suppressing or judging them, going along with them or even fighting them, we simply acknowledge they are there. Very quickly we will find that instead of being a slave to our feelings, we become an observer. We will accumulate less stress, increasing clarity will come and life will become much more comfortable, both for ourselves and those around us.

Gradually we can extend this practice to include our thoughts and, as we do so, newer and better patterns of thought will emerge. If we can take time out to sit quietly by ourselves and simply observe the mind and our feelings, we will develop increasing calmness and gain some insight into the mind and our true nature. This is a very good meditation we can do, particularly if we are already used to quiet sitting or have attained a little mental quietness. Over time we will become happier, more responsible and more compassionate. In short, we will become better human beings.

Self-improvement is a lifetime's work and there is no better education or way to fulfil one's potential than to truly know oneself. It all occurs in the magic of the present moment and the really wonderful thing is that it is an entirely selfless matter as we are contributing to making a better world. This is environmental friendliness at its best.

THE GREAT RESPONSIBILITY OF HAPPINESS

Having almost reached the end of our journey together, we should have an understanding or perhaps a vision of how we can be and how each of us has a responsibility to ourselves, to our loved ones and to the world. Love has the potential to bring us the greatest happiness and in doing so to make us into complete human beings. To possess a fiery heart is to become a peaceful warrior – a warrior who never needs do battle but whose presence heals and brings peace. Almost all human beings love at least a little, but a little is not enough. Each one of us needs to learn to love deeply and greatly; then we will live our full potential and give the greatest contribution we can to making this a better world.

The responsibility is immense and the learning curve steep – but the joy is boundless. The fire will blaze brightly in your heart, bringing you the greatest bliss, as the nectar of the heart sun, the elixir of love, overflows and fills your entire being.

{ APPENDIX

1. An easy and effective meditation

This is one of the simplest forms of meditation that can be done easily by anyone; it is sometimes known as *quiet sitting* and is a technique that rapidly induces a feeling of tranquillity. The mind is naturally drawn to movement and the key to this meditation is to allow the awareness to settle on a rhythm. In this case, the gentle rhythm of the breath provides a natural link between the body and the mind and, within minutes, the mind begins to settle; the breathing slows and the body becomes calmer.

When beginning with meditation, it is better to sit in a quiet place – a bedroom, study or garden, for example – but once we are familiar with the technique, it is perfectly feasible to practise it when there are other people around. Waiting areas in bus or railway stations and in airports are often noisy but can be good places to enjoy some inner quietness. Meditating when travelling can also help to reduce fatigue. Provided we are not listening out for an announcement and are not going to be disturbed by anyone directly speaking to us, it is possible to meditate anywhere.

People are often depicted meditating in one or other of the cross-legged poses, such as the lotus posture in which each foot rests on top of the opposite thigh. Such positions are not comfortable for most adult westerners, but if you are used to sitting in that way, you may wish to. For most of us, a chair will serve very well. Choose an upright chair if possible, and avoid crossing your legs at the knees – pressure on the nerves and blood vessels where the legs cross will increase as the body relaxes. Ensure that your feet are flat on the floor; this will help in maintaining alertness. Sit with the back reasonably straight and with the hands resting in the lap, or on the knees or thighs. It's important to be comfortable, but avoid slouching or lounging as these positions encourage drowsiness and won't produce the same benefit.

- *Place the awareness on the lower abdomen, just below the navel, and exhale. Feel the abdomen contract a little as you breathe out. As you breathe in, the abdomen will relax and expand slightly.*

- *Once you are used to the rhythm and the sensation of the breath, close the eyes and continue to breathe in and out normally. Thoughts will come and go. Don't mind them – simply be aware of the movement of the breath.*

Enjoy sitting like this for up to ten minutes. When you are ready to end the meditation, bring the awareness onto the whole body and take at least two more minutes before you open your eyes. Coming out of meditation slowly helps the body to adjust; you will have relaxed deeply and will notice the greatest benefit by taking your time to open your eyes. Once you have done so, it is good to sit for another minute or two with the eyes open before rising from your seat.

After meditation, you should have a feeling of quietness or calmness that will stay with you for some time. The benefits you will gain from meditation will build up with regular practice. If you can form the habit of meditating once or twice every day for ten minutes, you will notice a steadily increasing calmness and clarity in your daily activities.

2. Meditation to release tension: lotus in the heart

Some meditations utilise the imaginative power of the mind through visualisation. As a general rule, visualisation is easier when the mind is relatively quiet and settled, so before doing the following meditation it can be helpful to spend a few minutes of quiet sitting meditation, as outlined above.

In the *lotus in the heart* meditation, the awareness is maintained in what is sometimes termed the *heart centre*[24]

---

24 A focal point inside the middle of the chest, level with and slightly to the right of the physical heart.

and, by visualising an unfolding or opening of a flower[25] there, residual tension and constriction are eased. After using this technique over a period of time, many people find that they are happier and that feelings of loving kindness arise in them much more readily.

- *Begin by sitting easily, with eyes closed and the awareness lightly on the breath, as described above in the 'quiet sitting' meditation, for a minute or two (longer if you wish).*
- *When you are ready, bring the awareness to the middle of the chest – about level with the heart.*
- *Visualise at that point, just inside the body, a large flower bud. See it closed but with traces of deep pink or red showing through the green exterior.*
- *Over the next few minutes, see the bud open, and watch the petals of the flower unfurl. Continue watching until there is a fully opened bloom (it may be a lotus, lily, rose or whatever type of flower you wish). Imagine that the stamens in the middle are golden and that there is a beautiful fragrance wafting upwards.*

---

25 In theory, any unfolding shape could be used. The visualisation of a flower opening from a bud is very common traditionally, perhaps because the blossoming of flowers is a natural process we are all familiar with. In some teachings, the heart centre is said to resemble a lotus, which gradually opens its petals as progress towards enlightenment is made.

- *Picture rays of light radiating from the stamens and into the world around you, removing all suffering, wherever it may be present, and replacing it with comfort and healing.*

- *After a while, bring your focus back to the centre of the flower and visualise a small golden figure seated there. This image symbolises your higher self or spiritual nature – your inner potential and reality. Inwardly smile and feel totally at ease as you breathe in and out, maintaining a gentle focus on the figure.*

- *To close the meditation, let the visualisation dissolve or fade. Bring the awareness onto the whole body and sit quietly for a further minute or two before opening the eyes very slowly.*

3. *Quiet standing chi kung* [26]

This exercise is extraordinarily effective for settling body and mind. It involves standing quietly in a certain posture for several minutes, and is said to encourage the flow of chi in the body. Because the awareness or state of mind is important, this stance is sometimes described as standing meditation.

---

26 *Chi kung* (sometimes written *qi gong*) means "steadily working with chi", chi being the vital energy of the body. There are thousands of different chi kung exercises and routines.

The length of time is a matter of personal choice – three or four minutes will produce results, and you can increase that if you wish.[27]

- *Stand with the feet about shoulder-width apart. Turn the toes inwards slightly so that the feet point straight ahead, parallel to each other. This can be done by initially bringing some weight onto the ball of each foot and taking the heels out a little.*

- *The knees should be neither bent nor locked straight – just "soft". Stand with the back straight and loosen the shoulders by rolling them up, forwards and down two or three times. Allow the shoulders to relax and drop.*

- *Feel as though the head is being pulled gently upwards, as if by a thread. Tuck the chin in a little to straighten the neck and gaze steadily to the front, as though out to the horizon.*

- *Move the arms away from the side of the body – just a few inches – and turn the hands so that the palms face backwards. Bring the arms forwards a couple of inches, but be sure not to stiffen them. The hands should feel relaxed and as though they are hanging from the*

---

27 Although this exercise is easy, it is of a physical nature and may not be suitable for everyone. Seek advice from your physician if you have any health problems or haven't exercised for a while. If you have any doubts, or if standing causes you discomfort, it is better to refrain from doing it. In any event, only stand for as long as you feel completely comfortable.

wrists – it may help to shake them gently to release any tension.

- *Relax the abdomen and bring the awareness to a little below the navel – to the dan tian*[28] *– and breathe easily. As you inhale, the abdomen should push outwards. It will relax inwards on the exhalation.*
- *Feel the energy in your body settling. Whilst maintaining awareness of the breath, be fully conscious of your body and of the space immediately around you.*
- *If you notice your mind wandering, bring your attention back to the body and the breath. Allow the mind to become calm, without any forcing. Feel relaxed, strong and poised.*
- *When you have finished, gently move the shoulders, arms, hands, neck and legs, and walk around a little, to normalise circulation.*

As you progress with this exercise, you may occasionally notice slight movements or sensations as the body adjusts with the posture. You will also find that settling into the stance, mentally as well as physically, becomes easier and more satisfying as you gain experience.

---

28 A focal point just inside the body and about three finger-widths below the navel.

4. Open and close hands chi kung

All chi kung exercises are designed to increase vitality; most people experience a sense of inner balance and calmness as well as feeling invigorated after practising some chi kung. Most chi kung routines require concentration rather than physical skill and can be done easily by the majority of people. Within a short time of beginning to practise this exercise mindfully, many beginners experience growing steadiness and lightness in the body, often accompanied by feelings of warmth, or sometimes a pleasant tingling sensation, in the hands. Awareness of the body tends to increase, which can lead to improvements in posture, particularly when the exercise is performed in the standing position.

- *Stand with the feet about shoulder-width apart. Alternatively, if standing is difficult, sit upright with the back unsupported. Whichever position is adopted, the back should be straight and the head held up, as if suspended by a thread.*

- *Bring the hands up in front of the chest. The hands should be vertical and open, palms facing and slightly curved, as though holding a rather large grapefruit or a ball, with a small amount of space between the fingers. The fingertips on each hand should not quite touch those on the other, but there should be a good gap between the bases or heels of the hands – 20 centimetres or so is fine. The elbows should remain low and slightly away from the body, so that the arms are comfortable.*

- *Gaze at the space between the hands for a few moments. Imagine*[29] *that between the hands there is an energy-field or force-field holding the hands in place.*

- *Breathe in slowly and begin to separate the hands. Imagine that as the hands are pulled apart, the force-field is being stretched, like dough or elastic. As you breathe in, the elbows move outwards, allowing the ribcage to expand with the breath. The hands should be opened to about the width between the shoulders.*

- *Now begin to breathe out, slowly moving the hands back to their original position. This time, imagine that the force-field is being compressed between them.*

- *Continue slowly breathing in and out, moving the hands as described. At all times, keep focus on the area between the hands, noticing any sensations or feelings that arise.*

- *When you decide to stop (a couple of minutes will be plenty to begin with), lower the hands and hold them in front of the abdomen, just below the navel, for several breaths. End by lowering the hands, as though gently pushing downwards, exhaling as you do so.*

---

29 The imagination is used to focus the mind and is an important aspect of chi kung. It is said that the mind or awareness "leads the chi"; to put it another way, if the mind is focused, so is our energy and, with practice, the experience seems to validate this. There is much written about this; see, for example, *Qigong Meditation – Embryonic Breathing* Dr Yang, Jwing Ming, YMAA Publication Center.

SOME OTHER BOOKS THAT MAY BE OF INTEREST . . .

Ancient Wisdom, Modern World – Ethics for the New Millenium, HH Dalai Lama, Little, Brown and Company 1999, Abacus 2000

Awakening the Buddha Within, Lama Surya Das, Bantam Books 1997

Blessings of Bhutan, Ross and Blyth Carpenter, Hawaii University Press 2002

The Diamond That Cuts Through Illusion, Thich Nhat Hanh, Parallax Press 1992

The Great Little Book of Happiness – A Guide to Leading a Happier Life, Andrew Marshall, Radiant Sun Books 2008

Health Through Balance – An Introduction to Tibetan Medicine, Dr Yeshi Donden, ed. and transl. Jeffery Hopkins, Snow Lion Publications 1986

Journey of the Heart –The Path of Conscious Love, John Welwood, Harper Collins 1990

Meditation in Action, Chögyam Trungpa, Shambhala Publications 1996

The Meaning of Life, HH Dalai Lama, translated and edited by Jeffrey Hopkins, Wisdom Books 1989

The Miracle of Mindfulness – A Manual on Meditation, Thich Nhat Hanh, Beacon Press 1987

Peace Is Every Step – The Path of Mindfulness in Everyday Life, Thich Nhat Hanh, Bantam Books 1991 & Rider 1995

Qigong Meditation – Embryonic Breathing, Dr Yang, Jwing-Ming, YMAA Publication Center 2003

Textbook of Ayurveda – Volume 1 Fundamental Principles, Dr Vasant Lad, The Ayurvedic Press 2002

Tibetan Ayurveda, Robert Sachs, Inner Traditions 2001

Touching Peace, Thich Nhat Hanh, Parallax Press 1992

. . . AND ONE OR TWO WEBSITES

The Agni Yoga Society – teachings on evolution of consciousness: *www.agniyoga.org*

Articles and courses by the author: *www.joyousness.org, www.fieryheart.org*

Books, DVDs and other materials on Buddhism and related subjects: *www.wisdom-books.com*

The Mindfulness Bell magazine from the Community of Mindful Living: *www.iamhome.org*

Official website of His Holiness the Dalai Lama: *www.dalailama.com*

Sri Mata Amritanandamayi – an extraordinary example of love and devotion in service to humanity: *www.amma.org* and *www.amritapuri.org*